The Trinity

Hans-Werner Schroeder

The Trinity

Floris Books

Translated and slightly abridged by Eva Knausenberger

First published in 1986 in German by Verlag Urachhaus under the title
Dreieinigkeit und Dreifaltigkeit: vom Geheimnis der Trinität

First published in English in 2007

British Library CIP Data available

ISBN 978-086315-579-6

Printed in Great Britain
by Cromwell Press, Trowbridge

Contents

II Three in One and One in Three

III Dogma and Insight

Unless otherwise stated all quotations from the New Testament are from the translation by Jon Madsen (Floris Books 1994), and quotations from the Old Testamanet are from the Revised Standard Version.

Introduction

One of the most enigmatic doctrines of Christianity is the Trinity which states that in the highest divinity we have to distinguish three divine persons in one divine substance. This riddle has occupied the minds of theologians through the ages. Many conflicting opinions have divided the minds of those attempting to understand it. Wars have been fought in the defence of differing views of the nature of the Trinity.

It is hard for us to understand the fierceness and non-compromising stance of those who, in the early days of Christianity, thought and battled for acceptance of their particular concept of the Trinity.

For most people today the seems hardly worth a second thought. We may ponder perhaps fleetingly why Islam accuses Christians of polytheism with the claim that God is one and indivisible, and so could have no son. But would we enter into an argument about this? It is much easier to say, with a shrug of the shoulders, that we are not experts in the matter and anyway, why should we care?

With this book, which tries to shed light on the nature of the Trinity, an attempt is made to show that the concept of the 'Three in One' touches the very core of our humanity and our worldview; that indeed our understanding of the riddle is vital to our understanding of ourselves and the world around us.

The first part of the book addresses the persons of the Trinity: Father, Son and Holy Spirit. The second part addresses the difficult concept of 'Three in One and One in Three,' proceeding from the parts to the whole. In the third part a look into history will highlight possibilities for a new approach in our efforts to understand and experience the Trinity.

Father, Son and Spirit

Christianity is the only religion that sees a Trinity of the Father-God, the Son-God and the Spirit-God appearing as one. The Father-God is the Ground of all existence, the Son-God is created by him and the Spirit-God unites them (see also Chapter 5). Older mythologies and religious scripts allude to the existence of the trinitarian nature of the divine world as in India Brahma, Vishnu, Shiva, and in Egypt Osiris, Isis, Horus. We can perhaps understand them as forerunners to Christianity. While the Jewish faith does not explicitly mention the Trinity, we do find scenes in the Old Testament which allude to the Trinity and have indeed been interpreted as such.

In Genesis, for instance, God is mentioned in the plural form: Elohim. Though standard translations have largely chosen to ignore this plurality, we nevertheless find 'Let us make man in our image, after our likeness' (1:26). So we can see that even in the monotheistic tradition of the Jewish faith signs of differentiation and multiplicity have not been lost entirely and can actually be found in the Old Testament.

In the story of Abraham, when he is told that a son will be born to him, there is a change from singular to plural, which is quite evident to the careful reader. 'And the LORD appeared to him by the oaks of Mamre ... He lifted up his eyes and looked, and behold, three men stood in front of him' (Gen.18:1f). The change from singular to plural happens several times in the story and Christian scholars have long explained it as an allusion to the Trinity. The most famous of the Russian Icons, the

Icon of Rubliov, also called the 'Icon of the Trinity' depicts three angels as representatives of the Trinity.

In the three patriarchs themselves something of the character of the Trinity shines through. Abraham, the great father-figure of the Jewish people offers his 'only true son' as a sacrifice. The sacrifice is refused. His later son Jacob wrests the patrimonial legacy from his brother Esau by stealth. There is a similar triad in the three first kings: Saul, David and Solomon. Solomon, the third, is legendary for his wisdom.

In pre-Christian times the threefold nature of the divine world is not mentioned, with the exception of hidden allegories in mythology. Perhaps the time had not yet come for revelation of such profound mysteries, which were held by the highest initiates in the mystery schools as occult or hidden knowledge (we will look at the mysteries and the Old Testament in greater detail in Chapter 3).

With the arrival of Christ on earth however, things changed. The veil hiding the occult knowledge from public view was removed. Christ revealed the Father-God through the ministrations of the Holy Spirit and from then on everyone could participate in this mystery.

Even so, the New Testament does not reveal the mystery of the Trinity openly. Later on in the book it will be shown how in the first centuries of Christianity, the dynamic depictions in the Gospels, the letters of the Apostles and the Apocalypse, turned slowly into the rigid dogma of the Trinity. This *dogma* is the result of Church thinking mainly during the third to fifth centuries. The *truth* of the Trinity as a living presence in the New Testament can be found notably in the formulations of the Gospel of St John, as well as in the description of the Baptism in the Gospels of Matthew, Mark and Luke, and in the trinitarian presentations in the Letters of Paul and in the Apocalypse.

While there is no clear definition of the Trinity as such — the New Testament is not a textbook of systematic theology — the living presence of the work of the Father, the Son and the Holy Spirit is nevertheless open for all to see and experience, in much the same way as we get to know the threefold nature of the soul of another human being when we meet someone new and consciously discover their and our own feeling, thinking and will-impulses.

The ability to experience the Trinity through the New Testament has largely been lost in the course of the past centuries. Its place has been taken by a dogma, which is hardly understood any longer. The time has come to open doors to a new and re-enlivened understanding of the threefold nature of the divine world and the human being.

There will always be some things that are not yet open to our understanding. The truth of the Trinity is still a mystery, albeit an 'open mystery,' as Goethe called it. We will have to accept the challenge of a continued struggle in order to understand its depth and scope. It is important that we do this with reverence for the divine world.

Part I

Father, Son and Spirit

Who is God?

Contemplating the nature of God, we will of course first doubt whether an answer is even possible. Christian theology has maintained throughout the ages that God is beyond human thinking and experiencing and cannot be grasped in fullness by the human spirit; that indeed our capacity to know will reveal no more than can be grasped by human measure. God is hidden from view and his reality surpasses all human capacity to grasp.

Three main views have developed in time: God is invisible, unknowable and unutterable. God will always be that which is wholly 'other.' Human beings cannot make God an object of their understanding or experience. To know means to be in control of something. God the creator can never be controlled by his creature. Nevertheless, even the Catholic textbook* the above two statemens are taken from concedes that, while God is hidden to human knowing, he has revealed himself in depths of each one of us, through the revelation of his Son, through Christ's incarnation on earth.

We can conclude from this that the revelation of Christ,

* Johann Auer, Joseph Ratzinger, *Kleine Katholische Dogmatik*, Vol. 2, pp. 101, 104.

recorded in the New Testament, also holds the key to human understanding of God by and through his Son, who lived as a human being.

There is a further source of revelation, which has not found quite the same universal acceptance in contemporary theology as the first ones. Here the argument is: Why would God want to remain completely hidden from view? Should God not also be 'interested' in being known? Is it possible that he has strewn signs of his presence into and onto the world, so that human beings can discover them, if and when they choose to take up the challenge? Is it not asking the impossible of human beings to ask for their allegiance to God, that they love and obey him as the ultimate meaning of their lives, on the one hand, whilst on the other hand hiding the Creator from his creatures? Would God really want to play a game of hide-and-seek without leaving clues as to his whereabouts?

Of course we might ask: Have we been left without clues? Or are we free to seek for them? Since no one can be forced to do that, perhaps we have not looked to see what is hidden. Perhaps it is open to view all around us? Might unprejudiced observation point us in the direction of the Creator, when we feel free to observe him in and through his creation?

It is true that God does not appear as a person in front of us. But if we want to meet him, we can go to where he is, namely in his revelations. The revelations can and will open the door to the inner sanctum of God's dwelling.

St Paul puts it this way in his Letter to the Romans: 'For what can be known about God is plain to [the peoples of the world], because God has shown it to them. Ever since the creation of the world his invisible nature, namely, his eternal power and deity, has been clearly perceived in the things that have been made.' (1:19f RSV).

Naturally we must not fall into the opposite extreme when we go beyond the limited statements about the 'invisible God.' We are in danger of making God human-sized, when we depict him as an old bearded man, who rules the world with might and kindness from his throne on the clouds. Once we trivialize God, it becomes all too easy to reject him.

We can therefore also understand why theologians have spoken of the 'unknowable, the hidden God,' who is 'totally different,' and who cannot be grasped by worldly minds.

We must go further though. Should a world, which God created, not also have a visible divine signature? If we take it as true that God created human beings in his image, does this not suggest that there is a relationship between the Creator and his creation, which we might discover? Naturally not in the sense that we imagine God as a magnification of the human being, but rather that human existence and experience contain much which points to divine existence and experience, however immeasurably greater these of course are.

The purpose of this book is to explore the 'open mystery' from a human point of view, without diminishing the majesty and divine dimensions of God.

CHAPTER 1

The Father-God

The Ground of the World

The renewed sacraments of The Christian Community offer these words and images of the Father-God:

The Ground of the World
The Father-Ground of all existence
The Ground of existence of the heavens and of the earth
The Eternal Ground of all temporal existence.

The 'Ground': there is no other word, with the exception of 'Father,' that describes the being of the Father-God so fittingly. In the word 'ground' we see what is beneath everything, underpinning it; we see too the fertile soil, the ground from which everything springs; and we see the 'grounds', the reason for all existence.

The ever-changing, ever insecure world is grounded in his unshakable divine presence, which rests in and with itself, while an unending stream of creating life emanates from him. He is the eternal presence in all transitory manifestations, the eternal ground of all that exists in heaven and on earth.

First contemplation: the earth as Ground of Existence

We can all experience the ground under our feet. We take it for granted that the ground beneath our feet will carry us, is firm and safe enough to walk on. As we walk, the road changes, people change and the challenges diversify. And we are able to meet all these changes and transformations because we trust in the firm ground on which we walk, which will carry not only us but the changes as well.

Anyone who has experienced an earthquake we realizes how strongly feeling of certainty in life is bound up with our sense of physical stability. When the ground leaves us without anything to hold onto, we go into a state of shock. Fear arises within us, shaking us to the very core in the face of such loss of 'grounding.'

This experience of loss points to an experience so deep that we are not aware of it: that beneath all that changes in our existence, God is the safe, unshakable bedrock, upon which all creatures are safely held and carried.

Be thou a rock of refuge for me (Psalm 31:2)

My flesh and my heart may fail,
    but God is the rock of my heart
    and my portion for ever. (Psalm 73:26)

Such feelings may lead us to an experience of the Father-Ground; feelings of safety and being protected upon which we can ground our life.

There is nothing but God —
My life is in him,
He carries my whole being —
Both inner and the outer —
Never can I fall away from him

> He is the ground of my life —
> whatever comes my way —
> I will be safe in him.

Paul alludes to this truth in his speech to the Athenians, recalling the Greek poets: 'HE is not far from each one of us, for in HIM we live and weave and have our being' (Acts 17:27f).

Let us take another step. Let us imagine that the 'ground of all existence' is more than a formalized image, is more than a vessel holding and protecting the world, more than the bedrock under our feet.

Let us imagine that this divine being permeates everything; that it is in every particle down to the last atom of matter; that his being and substance stream into us in a living way, holding and enlivening us, as well as every part of the created world. Then we can say: his being is our being.

Not only can we say that he lives, weaves and is in us, we can also say that we live, weave and have our being in him. Our original relationship is twofold: I am because he is. And on this living experience I can create and build my relationship to him.

God the Almighty

The above thoughts give rise to the question whether God is truly almighty. One argument against the omnipotence of God is that he cannot undo what has been done. He cannot make 5 from 2 and 2. So he cannot be considered all that almighty!

But if we were to take the argument and stand it on its head, we might come to the question: What does 'almighty' mean in this context? 'Might' implies a power and durability as in the ground of existence. And if that is true for the ground, is it not all the more true for the One who made the ground and everything else?

Furthermore God made all the laws of nature and gave

human beings the means to discover them. God did not leave the world in a state of chaos, but he made order out of chaos. The order he created is for us to find out. The purpose of this order is that development may unfold, that chaos is held at bay.

Two qualities may emerge from this contemplation: the divine stillness and the towering majesty of God.

Second contemplation: divine stillness

We can experience these qualities in ourselves; for instance in the high mountains. On a clear day, the grandeur of the snow-capped peaks towering above us in their unmovable and unshakable silent splendour may fill us with awe as well as a sense of our own insignificance. An inner presentiment of eternal presence dawns within us, of its stillness and majesty, of the divine eternal unshakable ground. Once we have filled our souls with feelings of this kind we can recapture them; perhaps when evening falls and peace begins to reign around us. We can open to stillness and serenity, to the eternal embrace of the divine world in our feeling and experiencing.

Third contemplation: the stars

Life in the city makes it difficult to see stars. If we can find a place where the stars can be seen clearly, we see how from the velvety night-sky the stars shed their ethereal light. Feelings of awe and gratitude for their radiant majesty and peaceful movement open our heart and senses to eternal values; values that surpass our earth-bound human comprehension.

The starry sky observed on the oceans or in the desert, for instance, will become an unforgettable experience and memory, adding life to the mechanical, soulless images created by astronomers and modern science.

Such a memory can enliven the basic experience of the 'Father-Ground,' adding to our sense of cosmic reality of 'almightiness.' Eternity becomes an experience in view of the sheer size and majesty of the vaulting expanse above us. We can round the experience by contemplating the fact that the starry sky is not only above us, it is also below us and all around us. God is all around us. His hands hold and carry us, for 'in HIM we live and weave and have our being' (Acts 17:27f).

The living presence of God the Father is imprinted on all his creations; be it the starry sky or the immovable, unshakeable mountain range. They call us to awareness of his eternal presence.

Why is there something and not nothing?

There is another nuance of the word ground that we have preserved in English in the phrase 'the grounds for doing something,' meaning the deeper reason. If we have started to experience the Ground of Existence in a spiritualized experience of the dimensions of space, we can also begin to search for the reason — the grounds — for our existence in the dimensions of time. If God is truly the ground upon which we walk, where are we walking to? And where are we coming from? And what are the reasons for that? In the end we may arrive at the question puzzled over by the philosophers: why is there something and not nothing?

Answers have been given to this question along the lines of causality — the Big Bang as the beginning of a chain of reactions. For us, such answers will not suffice — they always leave another question unanswered, another link in the chain of cause and effect to be explained. If we take up the thought of God as the 'grounds' for existence, then we realize that he is the ultimate cause. Then we see that the world ultimately comes from God. The fact that something exists, and its nature, does not come from an amoral and meaningless evolution, which has no aim for its unfolding. The fact that there is a world, and the way the world is, comes from God's purposeful.

This view has an important consequence. A world whose final cause is in God does not merely carry traces of the divine creator; there dwell within it a divine meaning and a divine purpose, into whose nature we human beings can only gradually gain insight. Questions such as, does my life have meaning? Where do I come from, where am I going to? are all connected with this ultimate cause which is God. And it is our task to seek out the aims of creation, and to experience how our lives have a part to play in them.

The Christian relationship with nature

The thought of the origin of the world in God brings makes us look anew at the question of a Christian relationship to nature, for if nature has its origin in God, it cannot be without significance for us; it will in fact feel far closer to us, and all its manifold glories will be a reminder of the abundance of the God who created it.

In modern theology a new emphasis has emerged on the theology of creation, which had been sorely neglected. This comes as a response to the environmental crisis. However, it is hard for theologians in the mainstream of the Christian tradition to tread this path, as any attention to nature as a place of revelation is seen as 'heathen,' because in certain religions nature-gods were worshipped. We might ask, however, whether there was more to the ancient reverence of nature than mere idolatry and fetishism.

If Christian theologians had addressed the issue more creatively, if their view of nature had included the fact that its *origin* is divine, much of the exploitation and mutilation of the earth could have been avoided.

Humankind assumed mastery over nature, which we did not create in the first place, without accepting the task of stewardship, the task of honouring nature, by caring for what has been entrusted to us. The urgent need for every individual to step into the role of steward is becoming glaringly obvious. Meanwhile we kill what nurtures us without replacing it, without knowing how to create life anew.

A Christian view of nature will need to avoid two extremes: nature must not be confused with Godhead itself; nature is bound into the cycles of time, of waxing and waning; nature is not eternal. On the other hand, nature is not mere matter which has nothing to do with a God who is at work only in the soul.

Let us look at the latter thought more closely, through the following question.

Where does the substance of the world come from?

We have described God as the Ground of all Existence. Let us now look at matter as a manifestation of his creativity. Things do more than exist in general of course, they manifest in shapes and forms. And these shapes and forms are highly differentiated in terms of weight, resiliency, expandability, permeability, smell, colour and so forth. We find substances whose manifestations appear in material form, as for instance: gold, water, bones, oxygen and so forth. Substances fill the space within which they exist, from whence they reveal their presence. The human being for instance, reveals its presence through the substances of the body. Where then do these substances come from?

The explanation, which in time became dogma in the Catholic Church, was formulated by St Augustine in the late fourth century. In his view there is a dichotomy between God and World. God, Augustine said, is completely 'other than' the world, is indeed beyond involvement with anything as mundane as the existence of substances. God created the world 'out of nothing.' The substances that make up the world do not originate in God.

Our experience of the world and its substances expands immeasurably if we conceive of God as holding and permeating with his being everything in heaven and on earth, as bearing, ordering and permeating the invisible and visible, the spiritual as well as the physical worlds. Not that God needs these manifestations as proof for his existence, but his creations reveal his divine being, if we do but 'see' that the substances of the world have their origin in him.

It may be difficult to understand the world from this point of view. But does it not make more sense than to view the world as the result of random attraction of particles, atoms and molecules?

The scientific research of anthroposophy into the spiritual origins of the material-physical world strongly validates the hypothesis that spiritual states of being were transformed into material-physical substances in the course of evolution through processes of ever-increasing densification.

We are therefore called to add another dimension to our thinking: all aspects of the world originate in the Father-God, including its material components. The dogma of creation out of nothing can be amended, first formulated by St Athanasius and taken up by St Augustine.,.

The Father-God, much like all parents, gave of his divine substance to create our substance. Parents give of their substance in the creation of their children's substance. The child is their flesh and blood. And so it is that we can say: God's substance is our substance. Not only do I owe him my being in general, I owe him my physical existence in the here and now.

Fourth contemplation: spring

In spring we see most clearly the growth of the plants as they spring from the ground. A parallel image is our own growth, rooted in the Ground of Existence, the Father-God. Everything that grows springs from his essence and being.

It is the role of religion to deepen and expand the experience of what has so far been written here; and these are its basic elements. This is the basis of all prayers which turn to the Father-God.

Is God like a person?

'Every created being has its origin in God.' This could seem close to pantheism. Pantheists believe that God *is* every created being, and thus their view stands in opposition to those, who, like St Augustine, see no direct relationship between the created world and God, the eternal, majestic, unchangeable, who is uninvolved with temporal existence, since creating the world 'out of nothing.'

A third option may show the way between these two extremes: God is eternal, majestic, unchangeable and fundamentally unknowable as well as the ground from whence all things spring. Why should that be unthinkable? In everyday life we have the image of a mother giving of her substance to her newborn child. A tree can produce a myriad of seeds and scatter them without losing anything of its own essence and viability. In the same way we may think of God's being and substance at work in the world and in humanity, and thus have an inkling of his almightiness. God has a relationship to everything. He is not identical with his creation. He is greater than his creation. Indeed he holds 'all' in his hands.

How can I fathom such greatness in the face of my own apparent insignificance? Can I even hope that he will hear me when I try to speak to him?

We spoke of God as having had a reason and an aim for creating the world and the beings within it. The world, rather than having come about haphazardly, holds his meaning and purpose at the foundation of its existence.

And if in God is the origin of all that is, was and will be, it points to a divine will with an overall view we can only describe as being centred in him.

And it is here that his likeness in us comes more into view, because we also engage our will to decide and act with overview over the consequences. Our overview never has the same scope and magnitude, yet there is a likeness.

Can we even imagine that within his almighty greatness and unshakeable foundation, there is a caring concern for even the most insignificant of his creatures? The truth is that we cannot even imagine, let alone think that far.

We have reached the limits of our capacity to think and imagine. And at times our conscious capacities expand beyond their normally limited range. So for instance when a mother suddenly 'knows' that her son in another country is in danger; when pre-birth or after-death experiences dawn in our awareness, when, during life-threatening situations we suddenly see our entire life in pictures before our inner eye. We are unable by our own effort to produce such 'inner knowing' but there can be no doubt that such events point to the yet untapped capacity for knowledge and insight. The last example particularly is widely recognized by people who have survived life-threatening events.

Rudolf Steiner's research into the realities of the spiritual worlds revealed that the hierarchies of angels, who stand above human beings in their development, also have a much more comprehensive conscious overview than human beings. To know that makes it more readily understandable that we are capable of temporary expansion of consciousness, which for the angels is 'normal.' And the higher the rank of the angel, the more comprehensive and all-inclusive is their consciousness. We can have only a small inkling of God's all-embracing, all-holding, all-permeating consciousness as the signature of his divinity as well as our own potential to expand consciousness.

St Matthew's words bear this out: 'for your Father knows what you need before you ask HIM' (Matt.6:8).

God the Father

Christ himself spoke of God as Father on our behalf — of 'our Father.' May we follow him and do the same? May we feel the fatherly presence of the Father within us and in our lives?

Our considerations so far open the way to understanding ourselves as having been made 'in his image and of his substance.' In that sense he is our Father. Why would he not have a loving interest in his creation like any parent, whose love and interest are unconditionally there for their offspring? To imagine anything else is almost impossible.

Good parenting also requires of us to teach our children respect for their inheritance and to have stern words when we find them on a path of self-destruction. We do this because we love them and because we know more, and have a finer discernment of what benefits and what harms them. And we can feel in harmony with God, our Father, who also judges and punishes but always with the good of all creatures in mind. We can even understand evil in this context.

When the Apostle Paul said, 'in HIM we live and weave and have our being' (Acts 17:27f), he expressed something about our relationship to God. Here he does not mention God's relationship to us, but there is an implication that God lives, weaves and is in us, and that he has a fatherly interest in his creation.

Our Father

The prayer Christ taught his disciples addresses the Father-God with the words: 'When you pray, say this: Father, may your name be hallowed' (Luke 11:2). These words point to the divine reality in our lives and we can have trust in them. In this sense every earnest prayer is heard, because it is spoken trusting in the reality of the Divine. When we enter the reality of being heard, in prayer or in the sacraments, we enter ever more deeply into his divine presence in us. We can experience being seen and heard when we approach him. This experience can give us the certainty that our prayer is 'heard.' Whether what we pray for is granted is of secondary importance in the process, if we really enter into the words, 'Thy Will be done.'

The less space we leave in our prayers for egotistical motivations, the more room there is for the inner experience of his presence. Praying thus imbues our lives with the strength of his renewing power in spirit presence. That, in the end, is how our prayers are answered, when we find his 'voice' in us.

Our Father in heaven and on earth

Many people find it problematic to imagine God as a father, or as their own father. The image, left over from childhood, of an old, bearded man is also hardly helpful. For this reason, our first step was to develop a sense for the almighty, all-knowing, all-embracing power of the Godhead: God the Ground of all Existence, the ground we all spring from.

In the next step we tried to find a way to come into personal relationship with him, based on our inner experiences of his cosmic, fatherly dimensions. It is sadly true that in many lives the word 'father' fails to evoke feelings of loving, supportive or respectful togetherness. Many bear a marred father image as a result of pain inflicted rather than loving support given. Yet every child starts life with the wholehearted belief that its father can do everything. We might ask why that is — why is complete and unmitigated trust our starting point in life?

It is our heritage from the spiritual world: the experience of wholeness in love. Before birth we experienced the presence of the Father-God without any of the limitations of life on the earth. The time before birth is as long, as alive, as present, as rich and real as our life on earth. But before our life on earth begins, the world around us is permeated by the loving presence of the Father-God and the experience is still a present memory when we are born. We trust that the 'Father' can do everything and knows everything. And so we trust that we will find the same experience on earth in our birth-parent.

We all know that such trust is can often prove to be cruelly misplaced or even abused. It may take a long time, until we are much older, to learn that we can place our full trust only in the one Father of us all.

Starting with Ludwig Feuerbach in the nineteenth century, philosophers have suggested that the idea of God is nothing more than a projection of idealized human features onto an imaginary figure above us, stemming from the human need for security. The thoughts we have outlined above suggest something quite different: that each of us brings within us an archetype of the Father, which we seek in our life on earth.

The female aspect of the Godhead

Many people, especially women, are repelled by the association of 'Father' with 'patriarch.' Our egalitarian society has overcome the old dominance of the patriarchy: should not our religious imagery do the same? And it is indeed true that the father aspect of the Godhead in the Old Testament still stands in the foreground of Christian minds. God is depicted as the world-judge, whose judgment condemns or redeems. This god is in relentless pursuit of sins and the punishment of sinners. Martin Luther wrestled with the question: How can I find a merciful God?

The New Testament stresses other aspects and attributes of God, that were in fact present already in the Old Testament. His gentle, loving presence, which is perhaps a more female aspect. His lovingly embracing gentleness and forgiveness are revealed in Christ as attributes of the 'Father.' In the Revelation to St John we read that God himself 'will wipe away every tear from their eyes' (21:4).

And on a deeper level we can find a feminine aspect: Christ, the only begotten Son of the Father was born out of him. Here both the masculine, conceiving role and the feminine bearing are revealed in the Godhead. In God both the fatherly and the motherly aspects work harmoniously as one. In human beings they appear divided in male and female. There is no word in our modern languages that expresses this. God is both Father and Mother in One. Our challenge is always to add the motherly aspect when we here talk of the 'Father-God'.

He goes before us

The first sentence of the creed of The Christian Community states: 'An almighty divine being is the Ground of Existence of the heavens and of the earth, who goes before his creatures like a father.' We have already touched on some of the aspects. Now we will turn to the question of what it means that he 'goes before' us?

Aristotle spoke of God as the 'unmovable mover,' whose being remains eternally unchanged and unchangeable. Theologians have struggled with the question whether the biblical God does not in fact develop. Does not the fact that he sent his Son to live on earth signify divine movement?

'Going before' means two things. On the one hand, it means he leads us. Then, there is a temporal aspect: he precedes us, he was there first.

If we seek to understand these images, we can say that wherever we go and whatever we do, God was there before. I meet the divine presence in all the circumstances of my life, which he prepared for me. Furthermore, the eternal ground, which we saw in one light as the unshakeable ground of our being, *goes*. He moves in us, with us, through us, in all circumstances possible. He is the mover, the flow in all that is. To begin to grasp this in full we must combine the image of an eternal stillness with the life-giving movement of a stream.

Fifth contemplation: late summer

We can come closer to an experience of all this when we imagine the mood permeating late summer: the full ripeness of the fruit warming in the quiet stillness of a sunny day. A deep feeling of 'this is good' fills us. The sun itself streams around and into us, quietly warming, quietly ripening.

From the being of the Father-God flow quiet stillness and streaming love. From him flows eternal becoming, eternal being. Out of his being flows creation. Creation follows his creating, meeting his creating stream of life.

And it never ends; it is unchangeably changing in meeting all our needs for change and development in the course of time.

From the depths of his being the Father-God offers his eternal substance to become our substance. He is the source and the creator of all. In this sense we can say that he goes before us.

Summary

We have looked at motifs, experiences and images, which — though not complete — represent some aspects of the Father-God.

He is the Father-Ground, the 'rock' upon which the world is founded. We can come closer to experiencing 'God' in the unshakeable majesty of the high mountains, in the embracing quality of the starry night sky.

The quest for meaning of our existence led us to explore the 'ground' as both reason for and meaning of the sensory experiences of spring.

We looked at divinity as mother-father in order to explore our personal relationship to God.

And finally, with the first sentence of the creed, we explored the 'being' of God as eternally flowing creativity. We were helped in our experiencing by imagining a day of restful ripening in the warmth of a late summer day.

CHAPTER 2

The Son-God

From the Father to the Son

In the Christian faith God, the Father, has a Son. Why, we might ask, is the experience of God incomplete without the Son? Does Christianity need a Son to know the Father?

The beginning of an answer is already implicit in the name, Father. A son does not come into being without a father, and fatherhood only arises with the advent of a child.

The Christian experience is that God has fatherly qualities, above and beyond the majesty and power of the 'ruler of the world,' beyond being our father. Once again, we are asked to think of the most common of human experiences. To become a parent is a life-changing event in many ways. When we become parents we are challenged to be more open to change, to new duties and responsibilities, but also to new possibilities. The parental relationship we were born into is transformed and becomes more readily understandable when our own child arrives.

The fatherhood of God, supremely expressed in the Son, but implicit too in his relation to everything he has created, implies a change as well as his responsibility and duty in relation to the created world.

In his book, *Christianity and Islam,* Rudolf Frieling points out the innate incompleteness of a religion which denies the

Sonship, because such a God will remain eternally 'beyond knowing,' aloof and uninvolved.

As Christians we are able to forge a personal relationship to God by way of his Son. Furthermore, if God begets a Son, it shows that he is an interested and loving parent, who, beyond creating a son out of his own substance, also has a loving interest in the son's being and becoming.

Fatherhood on earth and in heaven means the nurture of development into selfhood and independence of the child. As parents we prepare the ground for our children's future and nurture them so that they can develop their potential and become partners in the life of the future.

The God as Father is interested in his creation and its future. Indeed he calls us into being as independent and free beings.

The Son of God embodies all these attributes in his own sovereign person, and is deeply united with his Father. As such he is the archetype of our own evolutionary development. In him is embodied the unity of the Creator with his creation.

We, as well as the Son, sprung from the Father's being and substance. We are born carrying in our being the same heritage of unity of the spiritual world and the earth. This finds expression initially in the unquestioned inner trust that my father can do everything and knows everything.

Christ's sovereignty, in profound unity with his Father, shows us the way to our inner sovereignty and unity with the Father. And we are free to follow him or not. While our 'grounding' in the Father is a given, our discipleship with the Son is a matter of free will and choice. Herein lies the core of the Christian worldview: the Father is involved with the Son, is lovingly interested in the Son and through him in us as son or daughter.

Many people find it hard to believe that God is interested in them personally. However, if we imagine the loving interest and deep concern of a father for his children, his delight when they become independent and creative beings in their own right, even surpassing what their father could do, we come close to the relationship of God to his creatures.

The Son becoming man

The fact that we have a separate existence on earth also means that we can have the experience of separateness from God. If we never separated we would not even begin to know ourselves as separate, or be able to step into not-knowing. The 'Fall into sin' is the fall into separateness, into selfhood, away from God's all-embracing presence. From a safe distance, human beings can face God and can face away from him.

What do we see when we face in the other direction? We come face to face with beings, who like Adam and Eve, somehow chose separateness over unity. And the longer we face these beings, the greater does the lure to be with them grow. The original Fall may lead us and them into ever increasing separateness; and it will do that, unless and until we recall that we are the ones who chose and are still able to choose.

If God chose for us then the wisdom of the experiment would fall flat along with our independence.

The Godhead chose instead to explore the reality of the human separateness on earth. God's Son took the path to becoming and being human, the same path human beings took after the Fall, which took us into ever increasing separateness from our original state. And while he was himself not involved in the Fall, he nevertheless consciously chose to experience what it meant and means to be human and separate, and also get to know the beings we see when we face in the other direction.

Paul wrote in the Letter to the Philippians:

> Be imbued with the same state of mind, which also filled
> Christ Jesus himself. For although he was of divine
> nature and form, he chose not to lay claim for himself to

be equal to God. Rather he emptied himself in offering and took on the form of a servant. In human form he took on body, and he showed himself in the form of a man throughout his whole life. Humbly and selflessly he submitted to the laws of earth-existence, even to the experience of death, the death on the cross. (Phil.2:5–8).

The poet Christian Morgenstern (1871–1914) wrote the following poem just before his death:

> Grasp in full this revelation!
> Turn your soul's gaze to the sun.
> Feel the bliss of God's creating,
> Filling every being there.
>
> And climb higher with the spirits,
> To the highest rank of all.
> You will find him, Lord of All
> Lord of all these spirit-beings.
>
> And then come to earth with him
> To humankind and to the demons
> Come with him to live embodied
> In a human shape with him.
>
> Try to feel the sacrifice
> Can your heart contain its measure?
> In exchange for heaven's mansions,
> God chose life in naked neediness.

Not only the death on Golgotha, but already his descent into incarnation on the earth was a sacrifice beyond measure. Only by becoming a human being could Christ touch the divine origin in the depth of our human being, which had become alienated from its origin. In being human, Christ becomes our brother.

The difference between the Father experience and the Son-experience lies in Christ's nearness and humanity. Rather than appearing in divine majesty, powerful and great, he appeared as a human being, descended to the human level, willing to shoulder all the weaknesses, all the experiences of loneliness and struggle facing us on earth. And so we can know that through Christ's deed of incarnation on earth God is with us in every possible circumstance of daily life. There is nothing he does not know and cannot feel from the human perspective.

We have quoted St Paul's words concerning the Father-God: 'in HIM we live and weave and have our being' (Acts 17:27f). Paul describes the inner experience of Christ with these words: 'So it is not I who live, but Christ lives in me. The life which I have now in my earthly incarnation I have through devotion and faith in the Son of God who loves me and has given himself for me.' (Gal.2:20).

In the divine Son, God comes near to us. He does not remain in the heights but comes in his Son who is our brother. God is now close to our hearts. He wants to be in the centre of our being. That is the meaning of Paul's words.

The Son became man

'He became man.' For many, such words are incomprehensible. It is indeed almost impossible to imagine God, the unfathomable, the almighty, in human form. Are we faced therefore with the choice of taking these words on faith, or of discarding them as nonsense? What are we to do with them? Simply accepting the incarnation of God on earth as a matter of faith and dogma can hardly lead into the depths or the magnitude of Christ's deed.

In the First Letter of John some of the inner experiences of the disciples who met Christ still reverberate: 'It was from the Beginning. We have heard it, we have seen it with our eyes, we have beheld it and touched it with our hands: the divine Word which bears all life within itself' (1John 1:1). These profound words cannot be understood unless we take the human being as our starting point. What is the human being in essence and in origin?

In the first chapter of the Old Testament we learn that God made the human being in his image. So we can safely say that there is indeed an original relationship between God and man. It is clear that this is an archetype, an ideal. How much of it do we find in ourselves and others, beyond perhaps the occasional glimpse? And yet, it was so in the beginning and is still true. In that sense we can say that the image, which we hold in the depth of our being as human essence, encompasses our yearning to be and become truly human. It is the image of God in us, and of us in God.

We may hold this to be true: that the essence of our humanity, the image we try to keep sacred in the depth of our heart's striving, for which we always yearn, has been thought into us and willed into us by God. In God it is a reality. He holds our divine being in his embrace while it appears in us on earth in a diminished form, made smaller to fit into our human form. In God the image of the human being is eternal, held safe in its original being. We have been, so to speak, crystallized out of the being of God. In every human being eternity is present, God is present; and everything that is truly human has in its essence the golden shimmer of eternal divinity.

If we are able to hold this to be true, it becomes less daunting to imagine God descending into human form.

God has something to do with us. We are, ideally speaking, the image of God. A possible translation of the words of the Gospel of John (1:11) is: 'He came into his own, into his property.' When Christ became a human being he came into something he was familiar with. And indeed, with his coming, the fallen and abused original image was restored. The words of Pilate proclaimed the truth: 'See, this is Man [*Ecce homo*]' (John 19:5).

We can but be in awe of the inner relationship between the story of the creation in Genesis and the New Testament. We are shown the story of a continued and continual creation. Through Christ, God re-enlivens the original image. He does not wipe it out, but endows it with new creative powers so that once again the shimmer of 'immortal diamond' can become visible.

Christ's deed re-establishes the original relationship. Through him it becomes a visible reality, and through him we are enabled to do the same, this time in full and conscious sovereignty of being and becoming.

God becoming man means that we can find the way to our own divinity and creatively grow into being truly human to become more and more one with Christ through our own deeds. As much as Christ chose the human form as abode on earth, we can choose to abide in him. We will not lose our independence but grow into it. That is the mystery of 'Christ in us.'

Christ, our brother

Through Christ, the divine world comes into an immediate relationship with the earth and humankind; and not just with those who want to be near to God, but with everyone. He shares our daily life, burdens, hopes, ideals, mistakes, weaknesses, errors and all.

The experience of the Son is completely different from the experience of the Father, just as our relationship with our birth father and our siblings is a different one. My father is the progenitor, unlike my brother who is of my generation and is therefore less complicated to be with.

In the words spoken during the burial ritual of The Christian Community, Christ is the 'immortal brother of mortal men.' He lives with us as brother and friend; he is the unseen companion of our earth existence. 'And see, I am in your midst all the days until the completion of earthly time' (Matt.28:20), and 'what you did to the least of my brothers, that you did for me' (Matt.25:40).

Such words are testimony to Christ's nearness, even to the degree that what we do to our 'brother' on earth we do to Christ. He calls himself our brother and even our friend in the Gospel of St John (15:14).

For human experience, the divine world has become immediate, almost tangible presence through Christ. The majestic, unshakable cosmic dimensions have personal dimensions in him.

How near is Christ?

How can he be near me, when I cannot feel his closeness? What kind of relationship are you talking about? Such questions are common, and they are easy to understand. Sometimes they are based on a false supposition, on the expectation that the experience of Christ will be overwhelming, accompanied by angels with trumpets. Perhaps Christ is so close to us that we hardly notice him. Many things are intimately close to us because they are in us. Yet we know little or nothing about them; so for instance our lungs, our heart, our nerves and so forth. Without them we would not be alive. Yet we are only marginally aware of their selfless and incessant work in support of our lives.

Can we think of Christ's presence in us being yet more intimate? We can think of him and know him as the heart within our heart, the breath within our breathing, the life-force in support of our life, the eye within our eye, the I within our I.

His relationship with us is a given; he is already in us, with us, and within us, which is where we can find and meet him. In the First Letter of John, the Apostle writes 'HE first loved us' (4:19). That we love him as much as he loves us is the path to his being and love.

What kind of proof do we want or need? Do we want a show manifesting his glory to convince us? If that were to happen we would probably be overwhelmed by our own sense of insignificance. The experience would leave us completely unfree to pursue our own life with any interest. Instead we would be over-whelmed by yearning for him. So where else can we look for his nearness to us, if not outside? Seek him 'in your heart' says the Apostle Paul. The Word of God 'is very near you; it is in your mouth and in your heart' (Rom.10:8).

We are of course utterly and entirely free not to want to know him at all anywhere. But if and when we do, we can begin by learning and experiencing what it means in truth to be a human being on earth and then go deeper and deeper into the experi-ence. He will meet us there on our journey to truth and love, as the brother and healer of our heart and soul's longing, and show us the way towards the 'Christ in us.'

Cross and Resurrection

In the process of going deeper and deeper into our own experi-ence of being truly, freely and consciously human, we can dis-cover our relationship with Christ, the 'heart of our hearts.' To contemplate this again and again can be like a ground note of our lives. But it would not be enough to stay at this level. We can only enjoy a friendship with another human being, spending time together, through sharing interests and experiences. Cultivating this kind of friendship is the next step of closeness to Christ.

We human beings have lost our original closeness to God. This brought us freedom, but it exposed us to the dangers of the adversary powers. This freedom is the foundation of a com-pletely free relationship to Christ. Nothing compels us to feel his closeness and his love; turning to him can only be a free deed.

On the other hand we see in our time ever more clearly the dangers that beset human beings when they come under the compulsive power of the adversaries. The abyss has opened up in our time, and we are in danger of a second 'fall' into this abyss.

Christ stands over against this power of the adversaries. He did not merely become man, but in his Passion he exposed himself to the power of the adversaries and overcame them.

The cross, his death on the cross, his resurrection on Easter morning, these are the marks of Christ They seek to confer on human beings the power to overcome evil. But to do this we need more than the relationship with Christ that is given to us unconsciously. We need a relationship that we have consciously sought. Then his presence can be more than comfort; it can become a power of *transformation*. Especially in moments of weakness, of loneliness, of suffering and despair, in all experiences of the dark night of the soul, of the threat of death and dying, seeds of a higher power can be found, a power of resurrection. Wherever the cross has been raised, we can feel, if ever so faintly, a new beginning, a transformation. This is the Easter experience of the soul.

There is a deeper dimension to human life, which remains hidden as long as we do not feel challenged. A serene and unruffled life seems a happy enough state to strive for. And so we expect, perhaps unconsciously, that Christ came to earth to make us happy, to solve all problems, that indeed he is the guarantor for our personal happiness; moreover that if we are not happy it is God's fault.

One of the greatest hindrances to personal development is this kind of thinking, which rests on the desire for personal 'salvation.' It fuels many religious movements and is a breeding ground for personal egotism.

It is an observable fact that we learn by overcoming adversity. The pain we experience in so many ways is an undeniable part of life and living. It is, so to speak, the cross we bear. It is also the healing agent, the transformative force in our lives. When we face the challenges facing us, they will reveal their transformative powers. If and when we face them, learn to deal with them fruitfully, we will benefit from knowing more than we did before. We will be transformed to a degree simply because we have more knowledge. Egotism would keep us from pain and suffering; it would also keep from us the transformative powers of challenges and pain.

Christ subjected himself consciously to all possible pains for the sake of our and his humanity. He accepted pain as a result of the Fall. He took the cross and carried it to Golgotha. His love imbued pain with life-giving transformative powers. And seen from that vantage point we can understand that his presence in our life does not mean absence of pain. It means that he shows us — if we allow it — the way to deal with pain consciously and lovingly so that death is no longer the result of pain, instead pain becomes an angel.

Christ did not promise an easy and pain free life to his disciples; indeed many of them gave their lives to follow and serve him. Acceptance of pain has purpose: it cleanses and transforms by burning egotism from our hearts. In the process it clears away the hindrances which prevent us from meeting Christ in our hearts, who did not deny the reality of having to deal with pain. For what benefit would we have from meeting him, however deeply, if we were not touched and transformed by his presence and his deed of changing the substance of pain into life-enhancing substances?

So the Fall we were involved in does not have to lead to death or to even greater estrangement from God. The transformative powers of the Christ have entered pain and form seeds for the future of humankind. And furthermore, human beings themselves are transformed through the transubstantiating powers of Christ. We can now be co-creators of our destiny rather than be subjected to it. We can reveal our origin as 'having been made in the image of God' through the new Christ-imbued substances.

In this context the Bible has two versions of the Creation. The first speaks of the human being made *in the image* of God (Gen.1:26). The second (Gen.2) speaks of the human being who has to strive to become the image of God.

Rather than reading both versions to mean the same thing, we can understand them to highlight the origin as well as the final goal of human becoming. They point to the fact that God made us in his image.

A true image of God cannot simply be a likeness without essence. If human beings are to be truly in the image of God, they must also have their own creativity, and must develop towards the ultimate perfection of the image. We are able to grow into his image with the help of Christ.

How Christ's presence in us can be of help in our destinies is still not altogether apparent. And yet the violently difficult events flooding the world can also bring us to search for Christ's transformative strength in us.

That we can truly find those strengths in us is documented in many biographies. An archetypal example is from the life of the poet Friedrich von Hardenberg, commonly known as Novalis (1772–1801). When Novalis was 25 years old he had an intense and intimate meeting with death and dying. Sofie Kuehn, the girl who meant more to him than life itself became ill and died at a very young age. Novalis was devastated. He descended into the 'dark night of the soul.'

'I am lonelier than loneliness itself, I am but a thought of misery.' With such words he describes his deep despondency, which brought him to death's door. And then came a transforming, enlightening experience — 'the fetter of birth became a bond of light' — awareness that death is not the ultimate boundary. 'Ask not whom I saw and whose hand He held, but I will perceive it eternally ...' At the grave of his loved one he had the experience of the resurrection at Easter. Christ had overcome death, imbued it with new life. Later on he wrote the following verse:

> I say to all mankind: he lives!
> He rose out of the grave.
> His dwelling now is in our midst
> For all eternity.

Ich sag' es jedem, daß er lebt,
und auferstanden ist,
daß er unter Menschen schwebt
und ewig bei uns ist ...

His words do more than repeat a Christian creed. They describe a personally experienced heart-feeling. Novalis never tires to tell the world of this meeting. He wrote about it in his celebrated *Hymns to the Night* and in *Songs to the Spirit.*

Novalis is a modern herald for the Christianity of the future. He describes the profoundly personal experience of meeting the risen Christ. He witnessed the reality of the resurrection.

The cosmic Christ

'Now all creative power in heaven and on earth has been given me.' These words at the end of St Matthew's Gospel reveal the other side of Christ, the side, which transcends the personal experiences we have had of him as brother and friend. They speak of his cosmic dimensions. The ritual in The Christian Community has these words: 'Christ, who bears and orders the life of the world ...'

While it is relatively easy to imagine the Child born in a stable and to experience him as brother and friend, a further dimension is his cosmic creative power.

The closeness we can experience is the result of his descent from the heights of his cosmic powers to earth, where he dwelled in unity with the Father. He then came to dwell in a human body. How can we imagine the long journey from being the Son of God to being the Son of Man? It was a long, unimaginably difficult and pain-filled sacrifice. Indeed we can imagine that his Passion did not begin in Holy Week, but long before then. In reality it began with the origin of human development.

The path he took from this beginning led him into birth on earth and into dying there. He rose from the grave having transformed human existence. After the resurrection he ascended through the heavenly spheres into the realm of the Father-God.

Thus Christ appears in the Apocalypse of John as the ascended Son of Man, holding the seven planets in his right hand, and his face shining like the sun (Rev.1:16). In other words: Christ carried the divine world with him as he descended to earth and carried the earthly world with him into the heavens at Ascension.

To our experience of his intimate closeness we can now add the infinite greatness of his cosmic reality. Both are available to us, though perhaps the latter is more difficult to fathom.

The renewed ritual of The Christian Community first leads to 'Christ in us,' to his closeness to us as a community. At the end of the Transubstantiation the view widens to encompass his cosmic-divine dimensions; during Communion bread and wine are offered as confirmation of 'Christ in us,' when we receive the body and the blood of Christ 'who bears and orders the life of the world.' He bears and orders our lives and destinies. Both go together. The first shows us God, the eternal stream of creation, God who is interested in each one of us and wants to be near us 'HE first loved us'(1John 4:19). No one is too insignificant to be loved by him. The other shows us that our life, however small, narrow or insignificant, is related to the all-encompassing life of the cosmos. Christ holds all in his hands — even our sins and shortcomings. He transforms and heals all.

Through Christ's ascension, his cosmic dimensions as well as his brotherly nearness are with us. 'I am in your midst all the days until the completion of earthly time' (Matt.28:20) 'And when I have been exalted above earthly existence, I will draw all human beings to me' (John 12:32).

So we can see that to Christ's holding and caring is added the bond of his eternally lasting nearness and love.

It is interesting to note that many people who have an experience of Christ today experience his cosmic dimensions as well.

One such witness, a woman, described: 'Out of the dark cross rose a light-filled cross which reached up to heaven.' The woman understood that what she saw was an image of Christ's deed of offering which opened awesome perspectives. 'I saw the cross standing between heaven and earth. It was like the hub around which the entire world turned. I saw the inner mystery of creation and of love.'

As part of the image of the Trinity, we understand the Father-Ground as the creator of all being and the Son-God as the source of all becoming. The Prologue of the Gospel of John says: 'All things came into being through him, and nothing of all that has come into being was made except through him' (John 1:3)

The eternal stillness of the majestic high mountains gives us the image of divine being, the world of the Father-God. Spring conjures up images of life unfolding. In the unfolding leaves, the new shoots, and the swelling flower-buds, we see promises of new life. We experience the wonder of becoming, the work of the Son-God. And such world-being and world-becoming is true for us as well, for all human being and all human becoming.

Nature is part of the world-being. It continues the old creation. The new creation, the world's ongoing evolution, depends on human endeavour. Christ's deed wakens humankind to envision and engender future becoming. Christ said: 'See, I make all things new!' (Rev.21:5) And he will do so through and with us.

Christ in the seasons and festivals of the year

The dual aspect of Christ can also be experienced in the Christian festivals in the course of the year as celebrations in memory of Christ and of his presence in us now and in the future.

At Christmas — especially during the twelve Holy Nights —

Christ truly touches each individual human being on earth anew, quietly and from inside the soul. Despite all the commercialization of Christmas, we can feel the enchantment, the magic of Christ's special nearness to us during this time. He is born again every Christmas as the brother of our humanity. His nearness works in us throughout the year.

During Lent Christ renews his Passion. Every year he renews his compassionate suffering with us through all the depths and abysses of our inner struggles. And in so doing he implants his power to overcome and transform into the hidden depths of soul, so that we too can overcome and transform pain and sorrow. Good Friday, Holy Saturday and Easter Sunday are more than festivals in memory of his passion and death. During these days Christ renews his deed of overcoming death. He imbues our struggles and sorrows with his power of resurrection, so that they may become seeds for future becoming.

While Christ is born again into our humanity at Christmas and renews his suffering with us at Easter, he unfolds anew his cosmic powers at Ascension and goes to the Father (John 16:28).

The image of Ascension is of Christ as he ascends and vanishes into the clouds. All the experiences of forlornness and sorrow, imbued with the strength to overcome and transform humanity and the earth, go with him to the Father. And so every year anew, the result of this compassionate and heartfelt human struggle becomes visible to the spiritual worlds. It becomes precious spiritual substance and is woven into the fabric of evolution. At St John's Tide this process culminates. Afterwards Christ renews his descent into the realm of the earth to be born again in us and with us at Christmas.

We can be his companions on the journey he takes on our behalf. We can experience his nearness and his cosmic dimensions in the course of the Christian festivals. He will then be near to our consciousness every step of the way. And furthermore we will participate in his earthly-cosmic work to the benefit of human and cosmic development.

In this way our participation in the course of the year is an inner symbol for continuing and continued becoming, made possible by Christ. He weaves in us, through us, in the Father and in the cosmos, uniting all again.

The resurrected body of Christ: masculine-feminine

We mentioned the female/male aspects of the Father-God. The same is of course true for the Son-God, the 'embodiment' of perfect harmony of both traits. In that respect it is interesting to note that in the first chapter of Genesis Adam is created male/female in harmonious unity. The division into male and female appears only with the creation of two separate beings out of the one (Gen.2).

Christ re-establishes the original unity through the resurrection. He reunites both female and male aspects in perfect harmony of the full human being. With the resurrected body Christ attains the future possibility of a united male/female — the new Adam.

Through Christ's becoming human, we are called to harmonize opposites in ourselves and to overcome the polarities at work in our souls. That is our task now and in the future. And the blood and body of Christ we receive during Communion is the seal of his promise that we are able to do that.

Summary

Let us take a look at the road we have travelled so far.

Father — Son — human being. The 'fatherly' aspect of God is established through the Son. The Son reveals the Father-God as seeing human beings as individuals rather than objects. Christ is the source of strength for individual development and evolution.

Christ becoming human. Human beings separated from their union with God and Christ made it possible for human beings to reunite with God when he became a human being. Becoming human is not a miracle, but a reunion, a re-membering of human beings with their origin, the image of God. By becoming human in all aspects, Christ the Son of God becomes the Son of Man and our human brother.

The cross and the resurrection. The gift of Christ's deep relationship with us allows a conscious and personal relationship with him, if we so choose. Sorrow and pain can be experienced as seeds that want to grow into organs to perceive Christ's resurrection and power of transformation. This power stands in opposition to death and evil and is our help on the path between death and evil. The path leads us into recognizing our origin and beyond this to being able to grasp our essential being as individuals without falling into separateness of egotism.

The cosmic might of Christ and the Christian festivals. Christ's cosmic dimensions need not be forgotten when we feel his nearness. Both aspects are celebrated in the Christian festivals. The world-creating might of the Father is revealed in the Son. In Christ, God's creative care for the world's evolution is manifest, which goes beyond nature into a new creation.

It becomes clear that without the coming of the Son the drama of human becoming is unthinkable. Much more can be said of course. But we now have a platform for our journey to understanding the Trinity.

CHAPTER 3

The Spirit-God

Wisdom and beauty in the world

In this chapter we explore the question, who is the Spirit-God and how can we understand the divine Spirit as part of God? Once again we will have to widen our perception and our understanding of the world.

The world receives its being and substance from the Father-God. The Son-God endows it with powers of creative becoming. The created world also manifests form and wise order. By considering the latter we approach the realm of the Spirit-God. Everything that shows wisdom, that is ordered and formed, is a manifestation of the Holy Sprit.

Wherever we turn, be it to the cosmos or the smallest particle, all things manifest meaningful order and creatively designed form. Though many astronomers consider the cosmos to be a conglomerate of materials in unexplored space, a look at the stars can show us the hand which ordered them; we can have an inkling that the patterns and constellations of the zodiac are more than images from mythology.

The fact that order and a kind of rationality are discernible in the world of the stars is increasingly accepted, even by modern scientists. Indeed the meaning of the Greek word *kosmos* is 'order,' order as opposed to chaos. The word conveys the conviction that the world is not a chaotic heap of matter; it does not move about haphazardly, and orderly development is possible and evident. In other words: the work of the Spirit of God, the Holy Spirit, manifests in the world. The Spirit impregnates being and becoming with order and creative design.

The world manifests the being and substance of the Father-God as well as the meaningful ordering creativity of his Holy Spirit. We are able to recognize the wisdom-filled order of and in all creation. The more we use our God-given talents of thinking, understanding and experiencing, the greater our capacity to recognize in creation its 'open secret.' This is the revelation of the Holy Spirit.

The Holy Spirit works and weaves in all forms and in all spatial dimensions: in the shapes and forms of the crystals, plants, animals, as well as in the formative forces of our bodies, in all organs and their functions. The Holy Spirit also works and weaves in all that develops in the course of time. He structures development and imbues it with order and meaningfulness.

There is a further element — that of harmony and beauty. The world is full of beauty and grace, even magnificence, which touches us for instance when we look at roses or lilies, or when we see a sunset, a small bird, or the face of a newborn child. Beauty is evident everywhere. And when such beauty, harmony and serenity touch our hearts, we feel the breath of the Holy Spirit, as he weaves in and through us.

So now we have considered three elements, which reveal the impulse-giving work of the Holy Spirit. He imbues creation first with order and creatively meaningful design, secondly with meaning and purpose in development, and finally with the formative gifts of beauty and grace.

The 'Holy' Spirit

It is a Christian tradition to speak of the divine spirit as the 'Holy Spirit.' What does 'holy' mean? The creed of The

Christian Community has a surprising explanation in the term 'healing' and 'health-bringing.' 'The birth of Jesus on earth is a working of the Holy Spirit.' And later: 'Through Christ can the Healing Spirit work.' Both terms stand in inner relationship to one another.

The Son who became a human being was — according to the dogma in the Catholic Church —conceived by the Holy Spirit. The Virgin Mary is his mother.

Let us add a few thoughts. The virginal, unsullied soul of Mary may also be understood to be the vessel for the fructifying presence of the Holy Spirit. Her clear, innocent purity enabled her to receive the Son of God during an act of human conception which involved Joseph, while her soul remained open to God, virginal and untouched by physical human passions. When we think in this way, the presence and working of the Holy Spirit does not preclude a human father.

So what does the presence of the Holy Spirit during the conception signify? We have seen wisdom-filled order and harmony of design as the working of the Holy Spirit. The fructifying, structuring power of the Holy Spirit ordered and prepared the ancestral line in preparation for the birth of the divine Son.

We can imagine that the body and being of Mary, the vessel for the incarnation of God on earth, necessarily had to be pure and 'divine,' unsullied by any of the destructive soul-forces human beings normally struggle with. Indeed, forty-two generations were prepared for the advent of the Messiah, in order for the highest form of spiritualization to take place in a human body. That is the work of the Father's holy Healing Spirit for the birth of his Son.

At all times — now as well as in the past and in the future — when meaningful order in life, beauty and harmony is created, it is an act against chaos and destruction and is indeed a working of the Healing Spirit, who heals humankind and the world.

The Healing Spirit in the sick world

The healing powers of the Healing Spirit have to be grasped by human beings from within; they have to be worked with in order to manifest sprit-working. Rather than working within the blood-line, in the genetic make-up of generations the Holy Spirit works as a healing agent for destiny.

To heal means to make whole, to restore something that is no longer whole. The original context is restored when healing takes place. This is the basic principle of the healing, restoring work of the Holy Sprit.

The world we see and experience is not whole any more. Many, many people live in dread of disaster and destruction. Why is that so? The answer comes to us when we begin to consider what being human means to most people and realize that in fact what we know about human beings is little more than we can see and touch. Conscious awareness, however, is not limited to the material components of the world. To exclude and ignore the soul-spiritual realities of human being and the world means to live with no more than half a reality. And there is the root of disaster: the inability to grasp both realities and unite them consciously in order to come to know the 'whole' reality.

A concept that excludes one half of reality increasingly leads to erroneous conclusions and reactions, so much so that, for instance, abuse of the natural environment and people on a global scale has become endemic. Once exclusion is at work it becomes easier in time to exclude other world-realities, such as the many facets of the soul-spiritual side of the global community overall. They are simply no longer included in our reckoning before we take action.

In a way it is good that the wounds of the world and its people are staring us in the face. We can no longer ignore the openly visible abyss filled with death and decay, brought about by materialistic thinking. A new consciousness has to evolve that is able to heal and include wholeness manifesting in beauty, harmony, ethical forms and true creativity.

The Healing Spirit works with and through human consciousness. He cannot work without it. Evolution, meaningful development, no longer happens without active human participation.

Sleep

The healing power of the Holy Spirit is present in the smallest matters of everyday life as well as in the greatest events. One example is sleeping. We take for granted that the state of unconsciousness in sleep refreshes us and replenishes our energy. We do not know what happens because we are unconscious of what takes place when we sleep. What refreshes and renews our energies, beyond the fact that our bodies rest?

When we sleep, our soul and life-energies enter the spiritual world and come into immediate relationship with the powers of spiritual beings who are at work in forming human destinies. We may not be aware of it, but that does not mean that it does not happen — after all, we know next to nothing about the inner workings of our body. Yet at times, for instance when we dream, we can have an inkling that we are neither truly unconscious nor inactive. Some of the night-experiences enter our consciousness, where they light up as truth-filled dreams.

Of course it can easily be said that this is pure speculation without scientific proof. However our experiences are proof. We need no scientific proof to know that we are loved by someone, when we have the experience of being loved. Observation will show whether we can trust our experience.

And on such a basis we can approach our sleeping and waking up. The capacity to be consciously open to learn more and know more about unconsciously experienced life-giving forces, can and will present us with experiences. From these we gain certainty that the Holy Spirit is at work within us, because experience is more convincing than speculation.

Our origins

Consideration of human origins opens a wider vista for our thinking about the Spirit. Are we descendants of highly evolved apes, or is this view also one-sided? Animals, however evolved and clever, live and survive through and by their drives and instincts. We do not find spiritual striving in the animal world. Animals do not 'think' beyond their subliminal drives for survival, food, shelter and raising their young.

Moral striving, decisions made consciously and lovingly, have no place in a world view placing human beings on the level of animals. Experience shows that it makes no sense to look for such qualities in animals. But if I consider myself to be a hairless, naked ape, no one can accuse me of being immoral, because I am true to my nature. I am not responsible for the consequences of my actions or the methods I use, because my sole concern is my own survival and that of my offspring. Precisely such subliminally held worldviews are at the root of decay in today's society, where idealism is scorned and spirituality is denied a place.

Let us ask a question. Does a teacher consider his students to be humanized animals that need to be trained, or are they individual ensouled beings who have the innate potential to be responsible adults, who need nurturing? Such a question makes abundantly clear our responsibility to nurture the ethical, moral side of our human being and becoming. The same considerations are true for all healing professions. A doctor's approach will naturally be influenced by their view of what they consider humane in medicine.

The entire scope of how we act and decide is influenced by the conscious or unconscious view of our origin. While it may be true that we have evolved physically like any earthly organism, from primitive to complex, the essence of being human is divine and has its origin in the divine world. Our soul and spirit do not have their origin in this world, but come from 'above' into the physical world. Our origin and the origin of all created beings is divine.

Nurturing and healing, the obvious aims of education and medicine, can only truly be effective when both the physical and the soul-spiritual aspects are addressed. An entirely justified and growing anger arises against education and medicine which treat people as soulless and spiritless organisms.

We cannot expect a materialistic world view to have the means truly to heal and to nurture. Instead we can expect more illness and destruction as our reasoning capacities succumb to such a view. Healing and nurture of the whole human being come from realm of the Healing Spirit.

Unholy spirits

Based on our considerations so far we may wonder, whether in contrast to the Holy Spirit there are other spirits less wholesome or indeed unholy? We have described some of the ills of modern society and of course there are many more, too numerous to mention. All of them have their roots in one-dimensional reasoning and thinking; the kind of thinking that excludes large parts of the world's reality from consideration.

Scientists rely almost entirely on knowledge gleaned from weighing, measuring, dissecting and speculating. Pure science has no use for anything outside this chosen domain. And thus life is not whole and we have to experience it as such.

It is not too difficult to imagine that behind world-healing as well as behind world-illness are world spirits whose powers to inspire evolutionary becoming as well as destruction manifest on earth. The human being, or more precisely human thinking, is the receptacle through which spirit-aims manifest. And we can know that the spiritual world is interested in human thinking for more than one reason. It makes it imperative that we in turn develop a thoughtful interest in the spiritual worlds and the beings therein. Needless to say, our thinking enables us to differentiate between holy and unholy spirits.

Thinking allows us to differentiate, to see what is not yet apparent to us, and to get to know the spiritual beings who — while inspiring us — hide behind the materialistic worldview. The progress of the world and humanity depends on such knowledge. Indeed it is of the greatest importance that we strive for it.

As has been mentioned before, the Fall separated us from God. In order for us to become free individuals, such separation was necessary. Through it, we became citizens of the earth. In order to reclaim our original state of wholeness we have to go where wholeness abides. We can freely choose to do so and we have the gift of the inspiring presence of the Healing Spirit within our thinking. It is up to us to use it in healing ways.

Simplicity and the complexity of thinking

While the materialistic world view captivates us with its simple logic, its focus is on matter to the exclusion of soul-spiritual realities. (The object to be researched determines the direction of scientific research. Since the creating mind of the object is not present to explain its meaning and purpose, it is much simpler to exclude the creator in the gathering of evidence.)

To highlight the point we considered human ancestral evolution in the previous chapter. The hypothesis that humans evolved from apes is logical, and is indeed supported by some empirical evidence. We are lured by the obvious simplicity of the reasons brought forth and are captivated by their logic. Yet the sheer simplicity invites and allows the exclusion of many other facets of human reality. We can see in the lure of simplification the unholy spirits working in opposition to the spirits of inclusiveness and healing. When we delve more deeply into the apparent simplicity of this argument we find that the evidence provided is a long way from proving that the apes were our physical ancestors. Indeed, there are indications to the contrary. Despite a multitude of details the real link to the apes has yet to be found.

And so the question of our origins leaves room for the discovery that human souls descended from the spiritual worlds to earth, into physical bodies. Two streams meet in our becoming human, an ascending stream and a descending one, a physical stream and a spiritual one. The ascending physical stream includes the animals (which are branches of human physical development). The other, descending stream, involves the human individuality, the spiritual identity, which in the course of evolution identified more and more with physical bodies suitable for a dwelling on earth. The human individual identity came from the periphery, linking over the course of time more closely to the physical forms as they became gradually more suitable dwelling for the spirit.

The same process is repeated from conception to adulthood. It is anything but simple. Two streams and their relationship have to be taken into account when human reality is considered. It is therefore not healthy to exclude one.

We can find proof through our thinking and experience. Can I think my origins to conform to evolutionary theories and myself to be the result of material conditions and energies? Or can I experience myself as a spirit-endowed individual on earth?

It takes considerably more effort to do the latter. And we owe much of the research in this field to the scientist of spiritual realities, to Rudolf Steiner. With anthroposophy, the world has been given safe and ethical tools with which to explore both streams in thought and in experience. The results are no less logical, no less convincing. And research conducted since Rudolf Steiner gave the results of his researches has gone far to show their truth. The healing impulses inspired by the anthroposophical worldview are obvious. Their creative, life-enhancing impulses manifest in many ways: in modern medicine; in both special needs and mainstream education; in agriculture, as well as in the artistic, social and religious culture of our time.

Steiner's methodology is exacting and requires strenuous inner activity of conscious observation in thinking and experiencing. The healing Spirit cannot work into our world without human effort.

Excluding human beings

We have highlighted the fact that materialistic thinking is detrimental; its short-sightedness lames and hinders human thinking and thereby human and world development. The space it accords to creative, moral, religious and ethical impulses is too small. We have also highlighted the irresponsible and disastrous results such thinking leads to.

Our worldview changes dramatically when thinking is opened to the spiritual, when it is enlightened by the light of the Healing Spirit. Here human beings are not without responsibility; they work and think creatively, because they live with the knowledge that they came from the world of the Spirit and will return to it. Human development is more than simply a random chain of causes and effects emanating from matter, but a process carried and cared for by the divine spirit. The impulses of the divine spirit live within human beings. Every night we relive them and they re-enliven us from within. When these impulses are taken up into consciousness, they will manifest their inherent enlivening powers in the world and in us.

We become aware of the inclusive and healing powers of the Holy Spirit when we include alongside physical reality the soul-spiritual, the moral and ethical components human beings have been endowed with. This kind of awareness will also allow discernment of the kinds of spirituality facing us at the moment.

In contrast to the latter, materialistic thinking engenders excluding thinking, feeling and habits. It infects the relationship between peoples and individuals as much as it affects the mood in the world; it affects the sense we make of events and how we run our lives. The effects are increasingly disastrous all around.

The author Georg Kühlewind once said that even if somehow a magic wand freed the world of all wars, all environmental pollution, all illness and unhappiness, all atomic and other war materials — in short everything that threatens us communally and individually — nothing would change unless the destructive nature of human thinking was transformed. The source of destruction is in the human mind, in human thinking, feeling and acting.

Healing will come from a transformation of moral attitudes, from healthy thinking habits, which enable the thinker to include and embrace the many facets of the world and humanity with care and respect. This kind of healing spirituality in thinking, feeling and acting leads to the source of healing and into the realm of the Healing Spirit.

The source of healing spirituality, or to be more exact, the question how the Holy Spirit actually works, has occupied the minds of theologians throughout the ages. Their answers have resulted in a schism between the Eastern and Western Churches.

The Holy Spirit from the Father or from the Son?

Theologians of the Eastern Church maintain that the Spirit 'proceeds' or goes out from the Father-God and that the Son is the mediator for the Holy Spirit. Theologians of the Western Church early on took the approach that the Spirit 'proceeds' from both Father and Son. In the fifth century this doctrine was formulated as an addition to the creed and became known as the *filioque* (Latin for 'and the Son'). These dogmatic differences of view lay at the root of the schism between the Churches.

It may seem scarcely credible to us today that such matters gave rise to great disputes. At that time however the Church Fathers were deeply involved in finding ways of understanding the Trinitarian nature of God.

Our observations so far are helpful when we try to follow the reasons for the schism: The Father-God creates the substance of the world from his substance: 'He is in all we are.' We meet him in all that *is* in the universe.

The Son-God is near us, in us and with us in the depths of our individual humanness. He stands with us when we are troubled and when despair grips us. He helps us to transform our being when we choose to work with his powers of transformation in our daily struggles.

How does this compare to the still current teachings in the Eastern Church, which state that the Holy Spirit 'proceeds' from the Father and only from him? We can understand the Eastern view when we consider the first of the three elements revealing the impulse-giving work of the Holy Spirit: order and harmony, creatively meaningful design (p. 54). We see them manifest in nature, in all the many wonders of the created world. Experiences and observations in nature pertain to the natural world and build an overall view. As such we can understand them as manifestations of the Holy Spirit who 'goes out' from the Father-God. To a large degree though, they exclude human individuality.

In the Western Church the second element soon joined the first one. Theologians experienced how the Holy Spirit inspires human creativity and originality as well as working in the natural world. The second element gained more and more acceptance. During the fifth century the *filioque* reached Spain and by the eighth century it had been accepted in Central Europe and Italy. The Church of Rome then declared it to be the sanctioned version of the creed.

We will be less surprised at these diverging views when we consider the historical differences in East and West. For the West placed a much greater value than the East on individual engagement in the social and artistic spheres.

The historical differences in the beginnings of Christianity show how the social and natural environment informed views and experiences. In the East the Holy Spirit 'going out' from the Father-God worked first through the world of nature to unfold creative spiritual capacities. He worked, so to speak, from the outside into the human soul. In the West, with the increasing acceptance that Christ's presence is the formative force in development, the Holy Spirit 'goes out' from Christ. He nourishes the growing individualization of human nature and works from the individual into the world.

When Christ begins his work on earth, he imbues humankind with his powers of 'I am,' so that 'I' can awaken to individual creativity through him.

'Through him can the Healing Spirit work.' These words from the creed in The Christian Community mirror the 'working' of the Christ Spirit in each individual human being as formative forces.

And so, once again, we become aware that the Holy Spirit cannot work without those human beings, who choose to align their capacities of heart and soul with the creative and renewing powers of the Son.

The Spirit working through Christ

So far we have considered how Christ's spiritual forming powers are at work in consciousness and knowledge. How does the human capacity to think and feel more deeply evolve so that we can fathom reality beyond the obvious? Human knowledge rests on the ability to gain through experience. Life experience forms our world view and life itself is the great informer.

To someone who has yet to experience pain or discomfort, certain dimensions of life will be unknown. A person who has experienced a great range of events and feelings will have the capacity to understand more and have deeper insights.

Christ works into the realm of our life and destiny within which we learn to understand life events and their meaning. His power to understand is our guide to understanding. Above all, as we have seen, he is with us when we are in great need, when we feel — as he did on the cross — that we are powerless and suffering. His understanding becomes our power to transform, with which we are guided through death into resurrection. In other words, with his understanding we do not simply suffer what destiny puts before us, but learn truly to grasp life's meaning and purpose. Christ's presence brings forth in us spirit-strength (the Holy Spirit's realm) to cope fruitfully and creatively.

Furthermore, as we seek Christ's presence in ourselves, new dimensions open in us for a deeper, more healing understanding of the world and its people.

Spirit-borne sacraments

When we want to feel Christ's nearness to us we can be specially helped by sacramental rituals. Here we may really be open to receive and feel deeply the light of his holy spirituality and his enlightening power in our knowing.

The nature and intent of Christian sacraments is to open human hearts and thoughts to the holy, healing spirit of Christ. The sacraments themselves are permeated by the radiance and light of the Holy Spirit. And so it is also important to consider the form of the rituals with the question: how well do they allow the spirit-substance to flow into those present?

As long as the Mass was celebrated in Latin, the healing light was obscured for human thinking because the words spoken carried meaning for the priest but not for most lay people. The new sacramental ritual of The Christian Community allows the spirit's light to shine forth in fullness from the words. Every word, every sentence carries specific aspects of Christ's deeds. Thoughts and words are permeated by Christ's spirit-activity and essence and his light shines through them. The basic formula, repeated throughout the Act of Consecration of Man (the renewed Mass), makes this clear, for it calls on

the *being* of the Father-God in us,

the *creating might* of the Son in us,

the *enlightening* by the Spirit in us.

These words could not more clearly reveal the meaning and substance of the sacrament to our understanding. They go beyond the old obscure formula: 'In the name of the Father, the Son and the Holy Spirit.'

The accompanying sign of the cross is a sign of our experience while the words themselves allow the light of the Spirit-God to enter our knowing. The words as well as the ritual itself address both realms of Christ's working: thinking and experience, which lead to understanding.

'Without spirit-borne sacramental rituals the human capacity to experience, think and understand, will deteriorate more and more.' Rudolf Steiner said these words to the founders of The Christian Community to underline the importance of the renewed sacraments. Human awareness of the healing spirit-presence of Christ will prevent such deterioration. Deeper understanding will deepen our capacity to understand life in its fullness. Christ's creating might in us will guide our thinking and knowing to choices in life, which include more than just abstract and superficial evidence. As we are healed and comforted, healing and comfort will be ours to give to others.

The Spirit, who 'proceeds' from the Father-God, also goes out from the Son-God.

Summary

We started our observations by considering the Holy Spirit's endowments first as manifestations in the created world — order and meaning as well as grace and beauty — in the realm of the Father-God; and secondly as the Son's imbuing our individual being with creative might.

The question, 'How does the healing Spirit work?' led us to consider healing in terms of the ills in the world. We found that thinking which excludes realities beyond the obvious produces illness. We considered going to sleep and waking up, and understanding human origins.

Unholy spirits work one-sidedly. Under their influence thinking becomes short-sighted and reactive, leading to exclusion of large parts of human reality. When we learn to include realities beyond the superficial, healing is the result. Deeper experiences also lead to deepened understanding that Christ, the Lord of our destiny, is our internal guide.

Christ also imbues the sacramental rituals with his spirit-light, where we can grasp it and begin to work with its healing qualities. Increasingly the Spirit reaches from the world of the Father-God into human individualities.

Creative thinking: the path to freedom

It is up to us to choose which spirituality we want to work with in our lives: we are free to choose. The path to becoming a free human being is described in the Gospel of St John (8:32), 'you will recognize the truth, and the truth will lead you to freedom.' Rudolf Steiner described the characteristic of the free human being as conscious awareness. Living creatively in conscious awareness enables us to focus on the wider and deeper meaning of life. The more consciously aware we are, the richer and more meaningful life will be. As long as we ignore the deeper meaning of life we are ensnared by everyday necessities and problems.

Christian Morgenstern put these thoughts into one of his last poems:

> Those who do not know the goal
> Have no way to guide them to it.
> Endlessly they run in circles
> Through a life without a purpose

> *Wer vom Ziel nicht weiß*
> *kann den Weg nicht haben,*
> *wird im selben Kreis,*
> *all sein Leben traben*

When we have a goal, we can pursue it in freedom. It is important to keep in mind that having an individual goal does not mean it has to be pursued blindly. It must not take us out of relationship with others or ourselves, but deepen these relationships into responsibility.

This is the highest achievement of the Spirit working in us: we are free to evolve. We are spiritually free to think creatively, to act out of spirit-awareness, and to be active participants in the future of the world.

Life has meaning

The knowledge that we can freely choose is supported by the insight that we are by no means insignificant for the evolution of the world. We are not products of random events, as the materialistic worldview suggests; we are not particles of dust floating in the universe through space and time.

The inner emptiness of such images leads to an inner emptiness in human beings, to hunger and thirst in the soul. And while they may appeal to logic, their one-sidedness starves us of — and indeed absolves us from — the need to feel responsibility, and the need to search for reason and meaning in life. As a product I am not responsible for my state of existence. As soon as I stop acting as if I were a product, I have to take active charge of my life, with responsibility for the outcome.

Thoughts and images of the wonder, the majesty, the grandeur and infinite order of the universe reflect the being of the Father-God to us. When we combine them with the image we have of ourselves as individualities, we enter the realm of the Spirit-God. Here we will initially feel more strongly our own insignificance, weakness and vulnerability; our life led in the face of death and decay as well as the results of materialistically-oriented beliefs and actions. Christ, who is our helper and guide, will not allow these feelings to overwhelm us. He will show the path to the discovery of eternal, divine values in us and in the world, which transcend material values in earthly existence. His eternal being can be in us. The Son of the Father-God will reveal to us our link with the Father-Ground of *all* existence. We are free to unite his Spirit with our spirituality and from there evolve into taking responsibility for the order and meaning of ourselves and the world around us.

Nietzsche's Superman

One of the most influential philosophers of the nineteenth century was Friedrich Nietzsche. During the flourishing of materialism Nietzsche experienced deeply the emptiness of the bourgeois society he lived in and began to search for greater dimensions in life. In *Thus Spoke Zarathustra,* he speaks of the *Übermensch,* variously translated as superman, overman, or trans-human being. In the Prologue Zarathustra speaks:

> *I teach you the Superman.* Man is something that should be overcome. What have you done to overcome him?
> All creatures hitherto have created something beyond themselves: and do you want to be the ebb of this great tide, and return to the animals rather than overcome man?

What is the ape to men? A laughing-stock or a painful embarrassment. And just so shall man be to the Superman: a laughing-stock or a painful embarrassment.

You have made your way from worm to man, and much in you is still worm. Once you were apes, and even now man is much more of an ape than any ape ...

Behold, I teach you the Superman.

The Superman is the meaning of the earth. Let your will say: The Superman *shall be* the meaning of the earth!

I entreat you, my brothers, *remain true to the earth,* and do not believe those who speak to you of superterrestrial hopes! They are poisoners, whether they know it or not.

They are despisers of life, atrophying and self-poisoned men, of whom the earth is weary: so let them be gone!

Once blasphemy against God was the greatest blasphemy, but God died, and thereupon these blasphemers died too. To blaspheme the earth is now the most dreadful offence, and to esteem the bowels of the Inscrutable more highly than the meaning of the earth ...

In truth, man is a polluted river. One must be a sea, to receive a polluted river and not be defiled.

Behold, I teach you the Superman: he is this sea, in him your great contempt can go under.

What is the greatest thing you can experience? It is the hour of the great contempt. The hour in which even your happiness grows loathsome to you, and your reason and your virtue also ...

The hour when you say: 'What good is my virtue? It has not yet driven me mad! How tired I am of my good and my evil! It is all poverty and dirt and a miserable ease!'

The hour when you say: 'What good is my justice? I do not see that I am fire and hot coals. But the just man is fire and hot coals!'

The hour when you say: 'What good is my pity? Is not pity the cross upon which he who loves man is nailed? But my pity is no crucifixion!'

Have you ever spoken thus? Have you ever cried thus? Ah, that I had heard you crying thus!

It is not your sin, but your moderation that cries to heaven, your very meanness in sinning cries to heaven!

Where is the lightning to lick you with its tongue? Where is the madness, with which you should be cleansed?

Behold, I teach the Superman: he is this lightning, he is this the madness!*

Nietzsche's words were deeply influential and found great receptivity. He connected the earth to the *Übermensch*. 'I entreat you, my brothers, remain true to the earth.' And we can say the same in the name of the new Christianity.

But from Nietzsche's words comes another, a warning sound: the *Übermensch* in connection with the *Unmensch*, the 'beast'.

'Man is evil' — all the wisest men have told me that to comfort me. Ah, if only it be true today! For evil is man's best strength.

'Man must grow better and more evil' — thus do *I* teach. The most evil is necessary for the Superman's best.

It may have been good for that preacher of the petty people to bear and suffer the sin of man. I, however, rejoice in great sin as my great *consolation*.

But these things are not said for long ears. Neither does every word belong in every mouth. They are subtle, remote things: sheep's hooves ought not to grasp for them!†

* Translated by R.J. Hollingdale, Penguin, pp. 41–43.

† As above, p. 299, 'Of the higher man.'

Rudolf Steiner quite radically analysed the trend of the nineteenth century and the experiences which led to such philosophies. While they are fascinating in that they uncover the emptiness of the values of that time, they also deny the reality of human existence; as if everything of value could be left behind in order to reach new heights. As such a high ideal is turned into an illusion.

We have mentioned the light of the Holy Spirit as the bridge between polarities, the bridge uniting the materialistic world-view manifesting as less than human, and the spirited-endowed human being. We can understand Nietzsche as someone who strove for spiritualized meaning. His *Übermensch*, however, became the antithesis to human reality, and as such unreal.

Harmony and equilibrium do not come about when human realities are ignored. The human reality is life lived between the polarities, between heaven and earth, between temporal and eternal existence. Our eternal being calls us to explore the realm of the healing spirit, who encompasses and unites both in harmony and equilibrium.

The topic was addressed by Rudolf Steiner with these words:

> Seek what is truly practical in life on earth.
> Seek it, but know its spirit-endowment.
> Seek the Spirit in life
> Seek him avoiding spiritual indulgence and self-focus.
> Seek him in selflessness while being practically
>   engaged with the world.
> And remember the age-old words: Matter is not without spirit, spirit is not without matter.
> Tell yourself: All that I do, I do in the light of the spirit.
>   I will seek the light of the spirit to warm all the
>   deeds of my everyday, practical life.

These words bring both together practical everyday struggles and the presence of the spirit. Seeking truth in the light of the Holy Spirit enables us to avoid mystical spiritual indulgence and self-centredness. It also calls us to understand our spiritual origins beyond our material orientation and from there explore the human capacity to be free.

To be free may to some mean freedom from responsibility, free to be irresponsible. Nietzsche's *Übermensch* does not lead anyone to freedom, but to the denial of responsibility. Without accountability, freedom is meaningless.

The creative human being is free

The inner experience of being free unfolds its full reality when we choose to be in the world creatively. We make use of our talents taking a real interest in the world, because we have these and many more talents. We are free to love. When we can love others, we are free to choose our actions accordingly.

The argument that we are not free as long as we are still tied to matter and that our love is dependent on sympathies or antipathies is not valid. To be free means to work, feel, think and, within the given limitations, to explore creatively how to do that without feeling hemmed in. With each individually creative act something new comes into being, something that has not been in the world before. Schiller described this in his *Letters on Aesthetics.*

As far as love is concerned, we give our love to someone for their sake, and not out of selfish reasons. This unconditional love is possible in every case through a genuine interest in the other.

Love is free. It arises from the love of knowledge. We can love our own destiny as well, when we place ourselves creatively into the world.

We have now returned to the starting point of this chapter: Through the guidance of the Holy Spirit we can recognize our own place in the world. Our contribution is our free and creatively chosen engagement with the world, which is necessary for its future.

Whitsun

In the Gospel of John (14:23) Christ says of the human being who loves him, 'my Father will love him, and we will come to him and dwell with him forever.' These words are read at Whitsun in The Christian Community. It is the message of the Holy Spirit; it is his promise to the world and humanity. The Father-God and the Son-God will dwell with and within us and the Holy Spirit is the uniting power.

The words of the Gospel also point to the highest divine manifestation within human beings. Love is the creative and world-embracing power of the divinity in us. We can awaken to love, to its creative powers and to Christ, who has his being in love.

The essential message of Whitsun is that we are free to become more of who we truly are, in a world emanating from the Spirit of love: 'we will come to him and dwell with him forever.' A vision and promise of the greatest possible magnitude!

Once we are able to understand and accept these words as true for us, our inner strength grows and opens our eyes for our true humanity. We can love the world, ourselves and our deeds freely. We can contribute to the future of the entire creation.

The image of the Spirit in light and flame

The 'Spirit' is the most elusive and most difficult part of the concept of the Trinity. To understand Christ as our brother is relatively easy in comparison to the world-creating almightiness of the Father-God. The word 'Father' however allows us to feel some kind of kindred relationship. What about the 'Spirit'?

How can we know 'the Holy Spirit,' revere and trust him? While we have been given images to help us, we must keep in mind that such images can never fully reveal his essence and character.

We have frequently spoken of the 'light' shed for instance by spiritualized thinking. And it is indeed possible to think of 'Spirit' as light. The essence of the Holy Spirit is light — radiant, clear-shining light — enlightening his realm of harmony, grace and beauty, which is without any trace of shadow or impurity. His realm is living wisdom. Every ray of light is a world-creating thought, the living power pulsing through the universe, much as the light of the sun penetrates and enlivens the earth's existence.

The New Testament has three further images: When Jesus is baptized, a dove appears; the image of the descending power of the Holy Spirit. At Whitsun the Holy Spirit descends onto the heads of the disciples as fiery tongues of flames. And John the Baptist says that Christ will baptize with the fire of the Holy Spirit.

The all-consuming mobility and aliveness of the flaming fire — the image of spirit activity — and the most radiantly pure light, both reveal the beauty, harmony and living, warming energy of the Holy Spirit. He warms, activates and enlightens our thinking, so that it does not remain cold and abstracted.

Imagine the light shining from colourful crystals or a pure diamond, whose incomparable fire brings a sparkling light to all its facets, and you have an image of light-filled clarity and fiery radiance — the essence of the Holy Spirit.

The image of the Spirit as a dove

It is perhaps more difficult to understand the image of the dove. In more ancient times, when images of animals were used to depict spiritual entities — the snake, the lamb, the composite sphinx or the mythical dragon, to name but a few — such images held occult meaning. In ancient Egypt even gods had the shape of animals.

Our relationship to the animal-world has of course changed over time, but in ancient times animals were symbols of wisdom and strength — the owl and lion for instance — or of demonic powers, like the snake or the dragon.

The dove, more precisely the white dove, was revered as a symbol of purity and holiness. Jewish sacrificial rituals endowed the unblemished white dove with the capacity to take human sins into the purifying fire of the sacrifice.

Birds live in the air and in the light. They are, by and large, creatures less subject to gravity than most. They freely move in air and light. We yearn for the same freedom of movement, to be able to rise above the bonds that tie us to the earth.

The dove itself represents the middle between the extremes; it is a creature of harmony. Doves are accomplished at flying, and they are also fast runners on the ground, unlike most birds, who are either good in the air while clumsy on the ground, or are so tied to the earth that they can no longer fly (like the ostrich). Doves are medium-sized, a medium between the great albatross and the tiny humming birds. The form of doves is harmonious. Other birds have inherent exaggerations, like the beak of a stork or the talons of an eagle. The plumage of doves is white, grey or light brown and always subdued. While doves do not sing like thrushes or nightingales, they also do not shriek, caw or crow noisily.

Erich Grimm wrote about doves:

> I would like to mention a not unusual experience, which shows the nature of the dove and its relationship to its environment. During the height of summer, nature is very quiet; few noises, hardly any bird-calls interrupt the contemplative mood of nature. The solitary soft call of the turtle dove, hidden in the foliage is the only sound; it is as if a loving mother were soothing her ill child with

gentle words, calming it, embracing it with healing warmth and sweetness. Nature itself 'makes whole' its fruits, which ripen in her embrace. Perhaps the doves tell us so?*

Another outstanding and characteristic faculty of the dove is its ability to orient itself in space and to find its way back to the place it came from.

We can see symbols of the Holy Spirit in every one of the dove's characteristics. It lives in the middle ground, is the intermediary between heaven and earth, between high and low. And as such the image of the dove adds its own dimension to the symbolism of flame and fire.

During the baptism in the Jordan the Holy Spirit descended like a dove. The gesture is significant and characteristic and most paintings show a dove with outstretched wings descending upon Jesus. The dove moves from heaven to earth, from the world of lightness and love into the earthly world with the aim of entering and permeating the actual physical form.

The old and the new creation

The description of Jesus' ministry in the New Testament begins with the baptism in the Jordan: the dove descends onto the person of Jesus standing in the river. In the Gospels of St Mark and St John, this forms the very beginning of the New Testament story. The Old Testament begins with a similar image: the hovering Spirit above the deep. It is the creation of the world and the *ruach Elohim* (spirit of God) 'rests above' the waters. The Hebrew word 'resting above' is used also for birds sitting on their eggs. And Hermann Beckh's translation, 'the Spirit of God lay brooding over the waters of the deep,' is a fitting image. The warmth of the brooding Spirit calls forth life.

* From 'Von der Turteltaube,' *Die Christengemeinschaft*, September 1974.

It is not far-fetched to see a relationship between both images, when we consider that the creative work of the Spirit continues in the New Testament. At the baptism, the Spirit appears over the waters of the River Jordan. His creative might now unites intimately with a human being. Creation continues and is renewed. The fire of the Holy Spirit, first introduced as 'brooding' warmth, becomes fiery spirit in the humanity of Jesus Christ. Indeed we may see these images in both the Old and the New Testament as a revelation of the Holy Spirit.

In anthroposophy the word 'Imagination' stands for a spiritual reality in the form of an image. In the image of the white dove the being of the Holy Spirit shines, whose warming embrace unites polarities, unites heavenly with earthly being, carries heavenly spirituality into human hearts; whose presence warms and enlightens human thinking. The Spirit-God's deed of offering for the love of human becoming was alluded to in the old Jewish rituals, where the white dove was first offered as a sacrifice—in a similar foreshadowing of the offering as took place when the sacrificial lamb foreshadowed Christ's sacrifice.

The image of the Holy Spirit in the wind

One important symbol of the Spirit has not been mentioned so far — the spiritual wind, or breath. In both the Old and the New Testament the words 'breath' and 'wind' refer to the Holy Spirit's presence.

In Hebrew, Greek and Latin the word for breath and wind are interchangeable with spirit *(ruach, pneuma, spiritus).*

We have an example in the conversation between Christ and Nicodemus. Christ speaks to Nicodemus about the rebirth through wind and water. Spiritual rebirth is possible only 'through the formative power of the water and the breath of the Spirit' (John 3:5). The dual meaning of *pneuma* is most apparent in the words 'the wind blows where it will.' It would be as right to translate: 'the spirit is present where it will.' Neither wind nor the spirit is predictable.

Imagine sailors on a becalmed sea, the sails hanging limply and the ship not moving. It is like a death-sentence. They can only hope and pray that wind will come up to carry them forward. The same is true for the spirit. He will be with us, even when we feel 'on a becalmed sea,' and comfort us with his inspirational power when we hope and pray.

As we mentioned earlier, Hermann Beckh translated the words of the creation as 'and the holy wind of the Spirit of God lay brooding above the waters of the primal deep ...' In this translation all three elements are united: The dove, the wind, the flame. 'Wind' speaks of the unpredictable and creative dynamics of the Spirit as well as of its invigorating nature which moves the air, and bringing fresh life-giving air, ridding it of toxic fumes and oppressive heaviness.

The Comforter

The unpredictable nature of the Spirit leads us finally to a passage in the Gospel of St John (Chapters 14 and 16), where the Holy Spirit is called the Paraclete — the Comforter, the giver of spirit-courage, the spirit of truth — who comes when we call on him.

Our prayers, our preparedness and inner readiness to receive him are prerequisites for the working presence of breath of the Spirit-God. The image of the disciples at Pentecost gathered together 'with shared devotion' in his name comes to mind. The working of the Spirit is a gift, an act of grace, irrespective of our efforts. At the moment when we feel least deserving and most in need the Paraclete, the Comforter, comes to us, when we call him.

In the Letter to the Romans (8:26) St Paul writes: 'Then the Spirit will stand in for us where our strength fails.' And we can experience again and again the gentle, embracing, loving presence of the Spirit-God when the light of spiritual insight comforts our seeking souls with understanding in making sense of life's events and destiny.

The individual and the community

One final aspect in our considerations of the divine Spirit of God requires a step which takes us beyond individual striving into understanding and supporting others in our life's community. The Spirit of God spans the space between the individual and the community. We can best understand this when we recall the first Whitsun festival. The mighty wind of the Spirit fills the entire house in which the disciples have gathered. The mighty wind becomes visible as fiery flames. The fire divides into small flames. Shaped like fiery tongues, they settle on the head of each one. Individual and individuating fire goes forth from the Spirit, who had come into the 'entire house.'

The miracle of Whitsun unfolds further. People who speak different languages find to their surprise that they can suddenly understand one another. All those who are present are able to accommodate their differences, each speaking in their own tongue, and simultaneously understanding the many other tongues, however foreign.

A legend tells us that afterwards each one of the twelve Apostles formed the experience into one sentence. The twelve sentences together became the new Christian creed. The legend reveals the meaning of Whitsun, namely that a new and deepened sense of community is built as a result of individual understanding and striving.

The Whitsun experience manifests as individual spirit-endowment. It brings a heightened sense of individuality, a sense which allows understanding of one's own individual purpose and of its meaning for the world's cosmic evolution. At the same time, the common divine origin of all creation is embraced, because suddenly I understand the uniqueness of every other 'I.' The individual 'I' is now free to acknowledge and support 'I am' in self and in others consciously and lovingly, and thus to enter into a new spiritual communion with humankind.

In our times we experience a radical striving for individuality and for self-realization in freedom from conventional restrictions. We can understand this as a developmental stage in the unfolding of individuality searching for new levels of individuation. The inherent danger to the individual as well as to society comes from the conflicts created when one 'I' feels it has to defend being 'I,' when the choice is either 'I' or the community. The resulting exclusion of either community or 'I,' leads people either to return to the group and be critical of the striving for individuation, or to bitter feelings of exclusion. These two are signs of the time. They manifest in violent gang-mentalities or as depression and even drug-use.

The truly free human 'I' does not have to make such choices. It is strong and selfless enough to honour and understand others in the community, and — on the basis of such understanding — to respect and nurture mutually life-supportive goals.

The ideal of the Church

In the past, the understanding and interpretation of the Holy Spirit (the creed of Whitsun) was solely the domain of the Church, which maintained that Christians could partake of the healing power of the Holy Spirit in as much as they partook in the services of the 'Holy Church.' The sole guardian of the path to 'healing and salvation' was the Church. For centuries Christians largely accepted the Church's guardianship, accepted that they themselves did not understand and therefore had to believe that their individual insights and interpretations had no place.

However, in the course of time such views increasingly conflicted with individual understanding and interpretation of the doctrines of Christianity. The Church's authority in questions of dogma was gradually eroded, and in the end attendance at formal church services began to fall.

The ideal of a church whose members feel free to nurture their individual spiritual cognition in a freely chosen community without any dogma, became a reality with the foundation of The Christian Community in 1922.

The common bond, the spirit of the community, is nurtured by the love and striving for spiritualized insight. The Healing Spirit of Christ — the healer of the individual as well as the community — comes to us if we prepare a place for him.

The life of the spirit in us is nurtured when we search for and live with love for healing spirituality in daily life. In The Christian Community such striving is supported.

The female aspect of the Spirit

We considered female aspects of the Father-God and the Son-God. It will therefore not be surprising that the same applies to the Spirit-God. The *Ecclesia*, the 'Holy Mother Church,' the representative of the Holy Spirit on earth — has long understood its role to be the mother, the nurturer of the human soul and human spirituality.

The soul's potential for spiritual cognition demonstrates how fit the image of the Virgin Mary is for this aspect of our soul-life. Mary, the mother of Jesus, is the incarnation of purity, grace, beauty and harmony of the soul — the female qualities of the Holy Spirit in their highest and purest form. Mary carries them within her and brings them into humanity in her purity, in her beauty of spirit.

A further mirror of the Holy Spirit is the divine Sophia (wisdom in Greek) who embodies dignity of soul, imaginative creativity and colour.

The Wisdom of Solomon in the Old Testament speaks of Sophia or wisdom as the divine co-creator, 'the fashioner of all things' (7:22) who sits 'by the throne of God' (9:4) and is the bringer of divine healing (7:27). Some medieval paintings show the Holy Spirit as a woman.

The Trinity has many and varied aspects. Male and female work in harmony co-creatively. Working with such spirituality evens the way for human beings to show their male or female strengths when the need arises, without polarization or pitting one against the other.

Much more could be said about individual aspects of the three persons of the Trinity, but we will devote the second part of the book to the exploration of its unity.

Part II

Three in One and One in Three

CHAPTER 4

The Unity of the Trinity

Three Gods or one God?

Normally we can imagine either one or three. It is rather more difficult to imagine three representing one, or one representing three. Indeed, through the ages the riddle of the Trinity has occupied thinkers to a considerable degree.

In the third and fourth centuries several solutions were offered ; two of them were extreme, several others lean to either side.

The first of the extreme views, tritheism, states that there are three gods, not just one. Tritheism led to accusations of polytheism or pantheism, the conception of the divine which sees it as identical with the created world. It was the great task of Judaism to overcome this view. In the context of the time it seemed important to hold on to one God, who, as one, is an unequivocal moral authority for his people. Tritheism would have jeopardized such a relationship.

Had tritheism been accepted, the accusation made by many Muslims, that the Trinity opens the door to pantheism would have been correct. The Christian Church distanced itself from tritheism in the fourth century.

Its place was taken by the other extreme, modalism. It states that there is but one God who manifests in various guises or 'masks,' depending on the circumstances, without being three different 'persons.' We are in much the same position today when we speak of the three 'aspects' of the godhead, without being clear about what is really meant.

The Christian Church weathered these controversies and also overcame modalism. It was not tenable because, as we have seen, the experience of the Father-God is unlike the experience of the Son-God or the Spirit-God. Christ, who became a Son on earth is very near to us as our heavenly brother. As such he is unlike the almighty Ground of all Existence or the Spirit-God, the wielding bearer of all wisdom and order.

It is a testimony of the inherent strength of Christianity that it accepted the Trinity as an ongoing riddle without a clear definition. Understanding the threefoldness and the unity of the Trinity relies on human experience, on wisdom and a sense for spiritual realities as well as divine revelation. The time has come when we can take steps beyond accepting such a doctrine on faith, and grow into conscious experience of the nature and essence of the Trinity, because we now have the capacity to do so.

The step from believing to knowing

The reality of the Trinity is to a degree still hidden from our everyday consciousness. It takes a spiritualized consciousness to fathom divine realities. The ancient clairvoyant consciousness that allowed human beings to see into the spiritual world has diminished further since the time of the early Christians. Its place has been taken by a focus on earth-bound reality. At the time of Christ and for a few centuries afterwards, human consciousness was still open enough to allow dim visions of the Trinity. In time it became less and less possible to grasp its spiritual dimensions and Christians became 'believers.'

It is important that we grasp clearly how we come to understanding: we understand something when we compare the new perception with something we already know. If for example, we perceive something in nature that we have never seen before, we cannot understand it if we find no parallels. Only when we compare it with something we know, do we find a bridge to reach understanding. With the help of the bridge we can fit the new experience into categories we already know, and then we feel sure that we have grasped the new phenomenon.

We have no way of understanding the resurrection of Christ, because there is no comparison. It is a singular, unique event without precedence. In order to even begin to understand the resurrection, we must find a bridge, a link to something we already know.

The same is true for the concept of the Trinity. The question is therefore, what will allow us to experience 'one in three' and 'three in one' and give us a basis for comparison.

Threeness

We can begin by exploring the principle of threefoldness. There is a threeness in the dimensions of space: above–below, right–left, front–behind. In time there is past, present and future. In human beings we have body, soul and spirit, and also thinking, feeling and will. And in the human body there is the rhythmic system, nerve-sense system, and the metabolic-limb system. We can also see it in the head, in forehead, eyes-nose and mouth-chin, and in the arm with upper arm, lower arm and hand. In our life there is life before birth, life on earth and life after death.

Threeness is an archetypal principle underlying the whole of creation. Even seven can be seen as a threeness of 3–1–3. (It is represented as such by the candles on the altar of The Christian Community.)

Looking for the principle of threeness will give us a ground of comparison and assure us that a triune of divine creativity works in the world and in us. The Trinity of Father, Son and Holy Sprit finds its mirror in the threeness of:

— Past (the Father), present (the Son), future (the Spirit)
— Body (the Father), soul (the Son) and spirit (the Spirit)
— Thinking (the realm of the Father), feeling (that of the Son),
    will (that of the Sprit).

The sacrament of Baptism in The Christian Community reflects the Trinity in the substances of water, ash and salt. The person to be baptized is touched on forehead, chin and chest in the name of the Father, the Son and the Holy Spirit.

So far we have looked at the Trinity as a threeness, but will now explore the unity of the three.

The principles mentioned above highlight differences within the unity in, for instance, the physical body. However, they make up *one* person. The distinctly different manifestations are the ingredients which together form the individual. If one of the three is excluded wholeness is lost.

When we now think of the body as an integral part of the human individuality, it becomes obvious that the bodily resurrection of Christ is of the utmost significance for the future of each individual, because it is the archetype for our future evolution. In the context of this book it is not possible to expand on this, but we can at least imagine a completely spiritualized body. We know that the body is a complete unit, functioning with the co-operation of all its parts. However, the parts in themselves do not make a whole.

The concept is a difficult one. As a rule we maintain that a body *is* the sum of its parts and can be dissected into its parts. As a concept this is indeed true, but only on a mechanical level. When we transfer the model onto the human being, we soon realize that the individuality is more than the sum of its parts and that dividing the parts damages the human physical wholeness. In that sense we can say that indeed the human being is 'put together' as body, soul, spirit, but the human being is more than the sum of those parts. We have been designed from wholeness for wholeness, and wholeness is not achieved by dissection.

Rather than thinking of the human being as being 'divided' into body, soul and spirit, we can think that the human being *is* body, soul and spirit and is yet more than the sum of its parts. In every part lives wholeness; wholeness is apparent and represented in each part.

The human being *is* 'body' and can be understood as such, as long as at the same time, soul and spirit shine through the body. Indeed the body is the vehicle for soul-spiritual work and deeds.

The human being *is* spirit and can be understood as such, as long as human physical and soul activities make room for the human spirit. We can have an inkling of what it means that the whole lives in the single parts, just as it is said of Christ that he is *one* part of the Trinity and yet the *whole* Godhead is manifest in him.

Three parts and the threefold whole

A picture puzzle is a conglomeration of parts. Lego parts can be put together to form a toy. The modern worldview holds that anything and everything is a product of atomic (or sub-atomic) particles. In school, children learn that $1 + 1 + 1 = 3$.

The ideas which underlie mechanical and technical work are, as we have seen, not applicable in the same way to the principles of being human, of life and the Trinity. Let us take another look at the human being. The human body has a head, a chest and limbs. The parts themselves have specific functions, which support and enable the other functions. They are alive only when they interrelate. The three parts working *together* make a functioning entity. But unless they *work* together as one, wholeness is not achieved.

In other words: the head is a head and as such not a chest or a limb. Both limb and chest systems are represented in parts of the head however: the mobility of the limb system is apparent in the chin and tongue; the inhaling-exhaling chest system is apparent in the area of mouth and nose; the nerve system is directed by the functions in the head. The equivalent is true for both other systems.

It becomes clear that the human being is highly differentiated and that understanding it requires intense and flexible thinking. Compartmentalization is useless in that regard, since it leads from the concept of threefoldness to fragmentation. Focus on fragments invariably leads to smaller and smaller fragments. Fragmentation loses sight of the life-principle of harmonious and co-operative unity. The living, flexible, creative view of the Trinity, threefoldness at work within human beings, makes demands on our thinking. And that is the characteristic of the Holy Spirit.

Rudolf Steiner gave a meditative verse which focuses on the three soul qualities weaving together to support human being and human life.

> *Ecce Homo*
>
> In the heart — the loom of Feeling,
> In the head — the light of Thinking,
> In the limbs — the strength of Will.
> Weaving of radiant Light,
> Strength of the Weaving,
> Light of the surging Strength:
>   Lo, this is Man!*
>
>
> *In dem Herzen webet Fühlen,*
> *In dem Haupte leuchtet Denken,*
> *In den Gliedern kraftet Wollen.*
> *Webendes Leuchten,*
> *Kraftendes Weben,*
> *Leuchtendes Kraften:*
>   *Das ist der Mensch.*

* *Verses and Meditations,* translated by George and Mary Adams.

The reader will by now have formed links between the concepts of triune and threefold. The mystery of the Trinity reveals itself to holistic thinking. It demands that we look at an organic threefoldness, as we have done with the human being. The simple method of division and combining of parts will not lead us forward.

The symbol most often used to depict the Trinity, the triangle with an eye in the middle, is inadequate; and so is the circle divided into three parts. Both are an image of division into three parts. Perhaps it is impossible to portray the Trinity geometrically.

In order to form a living image, we will now use an example from the realm of nature.

Threefoldness in the plant

All plants have three distinct parts. The Trinitarian archetype manifest in the three systems of root, stem-leaf and flower. In the seed lies the dormant essence of the plant. It is as if the parent-plant had withdrawn into the space of the seed. And from the seed it springs forth again as a visible threefold unity. This gives us a clear picture of the manifestation of the triune archetype.

We can now take a further step. According to the threefold principle, each single part of the plant holds within itself the creative essence of the other parts. This is evident in the flower which — with the forming of the seed — implants the potential for all three systems into the seed, so they can arise again when the seed is planted.

Even though the flower itself is neither stem nor root, mysteriously it is imbued with the essence of all three. Similarly the root 'knows,' even when the rest of the plant above ground is cut off, how to re-form a similar plant. How can it 'know' how to bring forth such a dissimilar parts, unless it is imbued with the archetype of its own kind? The threefold archetype of course also works in the stem: in certain conditions plant stems will grow roots. Even without an already existing root system, stems mature into flower and seeds.

We can see in the plant an example of threefoldness. Each part has the image and potential for the whole, and yet is unmistakably its own. We see a unity which at the same time manifests in a threeness.

The Trinity, an undivided triune

We mentioned the fact that when we come across something new and want to understand it, we unconsciously look for something to compare it with for which we already have a concept or picture.

The mystery of the Trinity has not been fully understood because it is very difficult to compare the Trinity with anything we know. Yet our considerations have shown that the meaning of the Trinity does not have to remain a closed book. Comparisons do exist for those who are not afraid to explore realms beyond the known boundaries, and have the courage to step into unfamiliar territory.

From this base we can, with greater confidence begin the journey of comparing and understanding, for instance, Christ in his full divinity without losing the particular manifestation of his being.

Just as in each part of the plant the other parts live without losing their particular identity, so we can imagine that *in* the Father, *in* the Son and *in* the Holy Spirit lives the threefoldness of the Trinity.

Christ's word, 'I and the Father are one' (John 10:30) does not mean he is the same as the father, but that his life reveals the creative life of the Father and the Holy Spirit.

'I AM the way and the truth and the life. No one finds the way to the Father but through me' (John 14:6). Christ is the way to the *Father*. *Truth* is the living power of the Holy Spirit, and the *life* is the element of the Son. Christ's words both describe the Trinity and are in themselves an aspect of the Trinity.

In understanding the mystery of the parts and the unity, we find a key to understanding not only the Trinity, but a universal principle.

The human being: separate, or part of the world

Let us take another look at the human being, with the above thoughts in mind. Do we understand our individuality to be a single, singular entity, or do we feel that we are one of the units that make up the world and its people? Our understanding of our selves determines our actions and decisions. If, as an equal member of the world and its people, I feel myself a member of a living entity, I will respond and act responsibly for the health of the whole living entity. If, however, I see myself solely as a single, unique individual and see the rest of the world and humanity as 'not I,' then my actions and decisions are nobody's business but my own. I may even feel that the world would be better off without all the others.

The moment we enter into a living relationship with the world and its people as one living entity within a living organism, we realize that we owe others all we are, that indeed my self is unthinkable without the interaction and presence of all the others. In the same way a rose is incomplete without root and stem, and a son is unthinkable without a father.

Our insights into the Trinity are a key to an inclusive and healthy understanding of ourselves in the world. Fragmentation obscures the view of the entity as a living organism. The view of the whole reveals the inherent purpose of the parts. A further step is our understanding that every one of us, every member of the created world, carries within the 'blueprint' of the whole. The macrocosm is in the microcosm and reveals the life and dimensions of the macrocosm to the discerning eye. Conversely the whole must relate to the parts. That means that the world is incomplete without the human being.

St Paul described the fact that everything which human beings do has an effect on the world around us. 'All around us creation waits with great longing that the sons of God shall begin to shine forth in mankind' (Rom.8:19).

When we begin to fathom macrocosmic dimensions as the meaning and ground of our lives, our microcosmic being experiences interdependence as mutually life-giving and life-supporting.

> Creation has become transitory, not through its own doing, but because of him who, being transitory himself, dragged it down with him, and therefore everything in it is full of longing for the future. For the breath of freedom will also waft through the kingdoms of creation; the tyranny of transitory existence will cease. When the sphere of the Spirit grows bright, unfreedom will be replaced by the freedom which is intended for all God's offspring. We know that the whole of creation suffers and sighs in the pangs of a new birth until the preset day. And not creation alone; although we have received the first fruits of the new Spirit, we, too, are painfully waiting for the secret of sonship which is to bring redemption right into our bodily nature. (Rom.8:20–23).

In regard to the social life, which joins us with other members of the human race, it will be more and more important that we re-member ourselves into membership with all of creation. Each and every created being in the universe is a vital member of the whole organism of life.

We can practice membership in smaller and larger communities. Rudolf Steiner gave the following words for this.

The healthy social life is found
When in the mirror of each human soul
The whole community finds its reflection,
And when in the community
The virtue of each one is living.*

*Heilsam is nur, wenn
Im Spiegel der Menschenseele
Sich bildet die ganze Gemeinschaft
Und in der Gemeinschaft
Lebet der Einzelseele Kraft.*

These considerations will give an inkling of the fact that the meaning of the Trinity far surpasses the scope of religion. It is as much the central creed of Christianity as it is the light revealing the hidden aspects of the world.

Three in one

We will now take a further step by looking into the secret of numbers. We have already mentioned the commonly applied mathematical formula: $1 + 1 + 1 = 3$. In this equation each unit is an equal part of three. Three is three times more than one.

Another and much older understanding of numbers looks at their qualities. Here 'one' is a unity, and it also contains all possibilities. One is all; one is universal; it is yet-to-be-differentiated potential.

The step from one to two is therefore a dramatic one. It is not simply a division into two equal parts; 'two' has separated from 'one' leading to a polarity. There is 'otherness,' inasmuch as 'two' has left the original oneness, and has segregated itself out of undifferentiated oneness into separate singleness. Exclusion

* *Verses and Meditations,* translated by George and Mary Adams.

from the wholeness of unity has occurred, and two is now experienced as being 'other than' one.

Three adds a further element in that it resolves the conflict between one and two by bridging the polarities, by including within it both one and two. The result is more than three; it is a new union, within which former polarities dissolve.

The example throws light on an aspect of the Trinity as the principle forming health-bestowing human relationships and evolution. We are not in polarity with the one God, but are included in his healing, divine will through its manifestation as the Trinity. Understanding the inclusive nature of the Trinity leads to understanding that we are not merely particles of, but participants in evolution. It requires inner movement and flexibility to find unity again.

Perhaps it is useful at this point to look at this principle at work in human thinking, feeling and will. We can see that healthy thinking, feeling and will come about only when all three work in harmony together. Will impulses, for instance, are instinctual and unbalanced without the input of thinking and feeling. Every human activity springs from a will-impulse. The outcome of the activity and its consequences is determined by the quality of thoughtfulness and feelings present in the choices we make. The same is true for feeling and thinking activities.

How human beings live within the harmony (or disharmony) of these three soul faculties, is determined by their strengths and weaknesses and is as free as they are. The consciousness which knows the soul faculties and guides and facilitates their healthy working together is called self-awareness. Spiritualized consciousness allows the Healing Spirit to bring about healing and harmony in us and in the world. (We can recall Rudolf Steiner's verse, 'Ecce Homo', p. 92.)

Bringing this to our understanding of the Trinity, we can say God is Father-God, but also Son and Spirit, without losing the identity of his 'person.' The Son has come to earth to reveal the divine relationship, the three-in-one and one-in-three. Even when we look at only one side of the divine, for instance the nearness of God, we can allow the other aspects of the Trinity to add to the experience, thus creating a higher, living entity. Then the majesty, beauty and healing power of the Christian image of the Trinity shines forth, and we see the ground of being in the Father, divine creativity and love in the Son, and divine, creative consciousness in the Holy Spirit.

The working together of the Trinity

'I and the Father are one' (John 10:30). We mentioned that these words of Christ highlight his spirit's unity with his Father's. It is not a numerical equation.

Imagine a rose. Each part — root, leaf and blossom — is something unique and separate. Nevertheless they each belong unmistakeably to the rose. In every part the nature of the rose is expressed. The nature of the rose is essentially one.

We are now in pursuit of a question which caused much debate among early Christian thinkers: Are the Son-God and the Father-God of the *same* nature or of *similar* nature? It was only possible to think of the unity of the divine Trinity if their nature was essentially similar. This was the argument between Athanasius and Arius in the fourth century where Athanasius' view prevailed. The resulting dogma stated that the Father and Son were essentially the same, the only difference being that the Father 'begot' the Son, and the Son was not Father.

How this could be understood was not explained, and it remained an abstract concept. How the reality of the Son's separate incarnation on earth could be brought together with an undifferentiated unity with the Father was inexplicable. This led to the truth about the Trinity becoming a dogma which could not be understood, and had to simply be believed.

However, today we have the means to think further without losing the unity of the Father and the Son. The Gospel of St John gives images which show that it is not simply an arithmetical unity. 'I am in the Father and the Father is in me' (14:10). And then: 'I AM the true vine and my Father is the vinedresser' (15:1). While the image of vine and vinedresser allows (unlike Athanasius) the difference between Father and Son, it also allows oneness of love, work and meaning to shine through. A further dimension is added with the words: 'I in the Father, and you in me and I in you' (John 14:20). Here we find instead of the Holy Spirit the human being mentioned as the third member of the Trinity. What does that tell us?

In these words the light of the union in spirit of Father, Son and human beings shines out, though at least for the latter the separate nature is obvious. Unity and separateness are not contradictory ideas in the Gospel of John.

St John not only points to the inner unity of the persons of the Trinity, but also on their working together. The most important elements are already mentioned in the Prologue (John 1:1f) .

> In the very beginning was the Word
> > [*logos* in Greek, *verbum* in Latin],
> and the Word was with God,
> and the Word was a divine Being.
> He was in the very beginning with God.

The opening is itself threefold. In order to shed more light into our considerations above, we can expand the parts.

1. The Father-God: In the very beginning was the Word.

Out of the Father-Ground of all Existence sprang forth the creative power of the Son, which may be likened to the creation of a word when human beings speak.

Through the Logos emanating from the Father, what is normally hidden in the depths of the Father is revealed. A creative activity arises out of the Father through the Son. It is interesting to note that for *logos* the Latin uses *verbum* meaning 'verb' and not *substantivum* meaning 'noun.'

2. The Son-God: and the Word was with God.

The Word (the son) born from the substance of the Father-God remained directed toward the Father, and in its creativity kept this relationship alive.

The Greek words *pros ton theon* ('with God') is not a static orientation (as in 'I stood in the room'), but a dynamic one (as in 'I went into the room') which is difficult to express in our language.

The first line refers to the origin of the Word as having come forth from the Father. The second line refers in turn to the Word's relationship to the Father.

3. The Spirit-God: and the Word was a divine Being.

Recognizing the Word, we see it in its divine nature: it is itself wholly and completely God.

Here a judgment is expressed, an understanding of the nature of the Son: when the light of the Spirit falls on the Son, his divinity is seen. The Spirit-God reveals the Son.

4. Summary of the Three in One: He was in the very beginning with God.

The divinity of the Word, spoken out of the depths of existence, was nevertheless right from the very beginning orientated towards the Father.

In a wonderful way the fourth line summarizes the three motifs into a unity. The image of the Trinity is already in the Prologue, apparent as a living, life-creating unity, which can be approached by the same dynamic human soul qualities.

The inner relationship of Son and Father is expressed in the coming forth of the Word. On a mundane level we can compare it to the experience we have when we long for words to express our fullness of heart. When we find the right words, it is as if by speaking with have given ourselves a new possibility of being — another aspect of ourselves comes to light.

In other passages St John tells us of 'begetting' the Son, and of 'giving birth,' and that out of the world of the Father something not only 'streams out,' is 'begotten' and 'is born,' but 'ripens' as with the power of the creative sun.

The second sentence of the Prologue speaks of the origin of the Son and his ongoing oneness of being 'with' the Father. In other words: the Word spoken by the Father does not leave the 'ownership' of the Father but speaks of and reveals the 'owner.' The Word reveals the harmony of being at one with his origin in all aspects of being, while revealing more than had been revealed before. St John uses the word *doxazo,* which has at its root what is *gloria* in Latin. The glory, the all-embracing Word-creating-power of the Father's love is revealed in the Son. The Father in turn reveals their unity in the power and glory of his Son's Resurrection and Ascension.

The harmony of 'being at one' of Father and Son is mentioned numerous times in the by St John. 'My Father works until now, and I also work' (5:17). And: 'The Father loves the Son and has given all existence into his hand' (3:35).

The verses complement each other. They reveal that the Father's creative work ('until now') has now also been given into the hands of the Son, of Christ. They reveal that with the coming of Christ to earth, the creative work of the Father as it was in the beginning — the foundation of life, our origin — can from now on be grasped on earth by the each individual human being through whom the Son can work.

In the previous chapter we looked at how the process moves from the Son-God to the Spirit-God. St John also points to this: 'I will pray the Father and HE will send you another Comforter, the giver of spirit-courage, who will be with you for this whole earthly aeon' (John 14:16f). With these words, divine working is entrusted to human thinking and working. So we understand how in the words 'I in the Father, and you in me and I in you' it is not the Spirit-God, but human beings who are included as the third element (John 14:20). Our goals, purposes, work and creativity can consciously unite in 'oneness of spirit' with the divine world of the Father and the Son. Human beings are included in the Trinitarian unity.

In the third part of the book the attempt will be made to follow the development of the conception of the Trinity through history.

Part III

Dogma and Insight

In the following three chapters of this book we will attempt to gain overview over past and present ideas about the Trinity. In the limited space available we will focus on the history of these ideas, and on the results of spiritual-scientific research into the topic, which has led a renewal of religious life and thinking. While many details will only be touched upon, they may deepen and clarify what has already been said so far.

CHAPTER 5

The Trinity in History

The concept of the Trinity is Christian, and was unknown in the ancient world. Yet there are traces to be found in the mythologies of the pre-Christian cultures, which indicate that the knowledge of the Trinity was cared for in mystery centres and from there flowed into myths and legends in the form of images.

Mythological images

Three was a holy number in many old cultures, widely used as a religious symbol. Babylonian mysteries spoke of a threefold earth in a threefold heaven: the sky in the highest heaven, the earth in heavenly earth and the sea in a heavenly ocean.

In many ancient religions and mythologies the divine triad, a trinity of gods, played a major part. In India the highest divinity, Trimurti, has three aspects: Vishnu, Brahma, and Shiva. The ritual involved three sacramental fires: Garhapatya is the central fire, Ahavaniya is the western fire and Anvaharyapacana is the fire in the east.

Especially remarkable is the triad of gods in Egypt. It seems directly to prefigure Christianity. The father-god is Osiris, the mother-goddess is Isis and the son-god is Horus. The place of the Holy Spirit is taken by the mother-goddess, a place which later on in Christianity is taken by Mary, the mother of Jesus or Mary-Sophia, the incarnation of spiritualized wisdom. The pattern of father, mother and son is found in the ancient Egyptian capital of Memphis. Ptah is the male god, Sekhmet is the lion-headed goddess and Nefertem is the young god who carries a lotus flower on his head. In Babylonia there is also the triad of Anu, Enlil and Ea or Enki, and of Sin, Ishtar and Shamash.

The triad of gods continues to play a role in Greece. Hades, Poseidon and Zeus rule together. There are also the three judges of death — Minos, Aiakos and Rhadamanthys — and the three Gorgons — Sthenno, Euryale and Medusa — the three Horae — Eunomia, Diké, and Eirene — the three Fates — Clotho, Lachesis and Atropos, and the three Graces — Aglaia, Euphrosyne and Thalia.

The Germanic tribes worshipped Odin (or Wodan), Frigg (or Frikke) and Thor. In Germanic mythology there are many triads such as those of giants, of fates, of the realms of the gods and those of earth.

In Northern France carved stone images have been found showing a person with three heads and three faces.

The list could be continued with examples from other mythologies. The above though shows a plethora of triads and images, which may be understood to be precursors to the future revelations of the highest truth of Christianity.

The triad of images also appears in the fairy tales, in the king, his son and the princess who has to be saved from dark powers. There are often three sons or three brothers, three wishes, three tasks and so forth.

The mysteries in antiquity

The mystery centres of antiquity were the guardians of esoteric wisdom, and in all likelihood had knowledge of the Trinitarian secrets. All ancient cultures had mystery schools which taught esoteric knowledge, initiated students into seeing and experiencing the secrets of the divine world.

Some names of the mystery schools are still known, such as

Eleusis and Samothrace. The Mithraic mystery was still in place in the early days of Christianity. Little was written about the mysteries, since betrayal of their secrets was punishable by death. Yet even the little that is still available shows knowledge of the Trinity. The Church Father Hippolytus mentioned one of the central events celebrated in the mystery of Eleusis. He describes how a great fire was lit during the night before the initiation was to take place. The hierophant celebrating unutterable, deep secrets proclaimed in a loud voice: 'A holy boy has been born to her who rules; Brimo bore Brimos, that is from Strength comes forth the Strong one.' Reputedly the celebrations were accompanied by visions, *epopteia*, of the Mother and her Son, which of course implies the generative presence of the Father. Names of mystical triads in and around the Eleusian mysteries were Demeter, Koré (or Persephone) and Triptolemos. (From Eleusis also came the fabled marble triptych of the fifth century BC.) Other variations of the theme were Thea (Perspeia), Theos (Pluto) and Eubulos.

Of the Mithraic mysteries Kerenyi writes the following:

> Aside from the triad of Mithras with the two Dadophores, other archaeological finds point to the significance of Trinity in the Mithraic mystery schools. The most remarkable among them is found in the church at Dieburg, Germany, on the right-hand side of the altar picture. We see a tree trunk with three branches. Each branch has a head with a Phrygian hat. The same motive can be seen on an altar stone in Rückingen, Germany.

Similarly, the highest three grades of the seven stages of initiation: the 'Persian,' the Sun-Hero and the Father are related to the Trinity. The highest grade, the Father, even names the principle of the Father-God, while through the name Sun-Hero shines Christ's sun-relatedness. The fifth grade, the Persian (the name changed from nation to nation), shows the spiritual relatedness of the initiate to the spiritual entity of a particular people — an aspect of the Holy Spirit.

In *Christianity as a Mystical Fact*, Rudolf Steiner writes about the pre-Christian mystery schools and their preparatory role for the incarnation of the Son on the earth. Rudolf Steiner's spiritual research uncovered the wisdom of the initiating practices and their meaning and influence. He helps us to understand that knowledge of the Trinity is the content and the purpose of the mystery schools. He points out that they were in the truest sense 'established' by the Holy Spirit, by his wise and inspirational presence in human beings. They were 'mysteries of the Spirit.'

In many ways, their content anticipated the content of Christianity, prophesying Christ's nearness. Death and resurrection were central practices in the ancient mysteries. The death-experience, lasting three days, was a state of sleep, not unlike an actual death, followed by 'awakening' through the hierophant who had the highest initiate grade of Father.

The same principle was at work in the Adonis festival: the 'death' of a god was celebrated annually as well as the resurrection of the divinity. The myth of Osiris is similar. The central motif is the 'birth of the Son' in all cases.

Rudolf Steiner said that before the birth of Christ in various mystery centres initiates of the Holy Spirit had become aware of the approach of the Son, the Messiah, to the realm of earth.

Knowledge of the 'coming Son' was possible when the sixth grade of initiation, the Sun-Hero, had been attained. It is a grade of initiation in which the initiate could 'live in the universe and know the spiritual nature of the stars. At this stage the candidate became on of the resurrected and could observe the forces of the moon and sun at work, particularly in their effects upon earthly humanity.'*

* *The Easter Festival in the Evolution of the Mysteries,* lecture of April 20, 1924.

The highest grade of initiation, the Father, endowed the bearer with the strength of heart and soul actually to be a father in the most exalted sense of the word, and to the neophytes who entered the mystery centre, he became the human representative of the Father-God.

> ... something entered into [the initiate] through the sacred enactments in the mysteries, something which had been felt and experienced in all ancient civilizations as the eternal Father in the cosmos. And when the initiate, the mystic, had reached a certain point of his initiation in the ancient mysteries he had an experience that allowed him to say to himself ...: The Father lives in me.*

Rudolf Steiner's insights make clear that in the ancient mystery schools, knowledge of the Trinity was alive, nurtured and experienced. The highest grades of initiation led into a full experience of the reality of the Trinity.

Practice and content of the mystery schools was sacred, esoteric knowledge, not to be divulged to profane minds. The esoteric content was, however, disseminated in symbols, myths and images and flowed into the sacramental religion of the people in the world.

With Christianity, the secrets of the mysteries come into public view. When the light in the ancient mysteries united with the light of Christianity, the truth of the Trinity became 'an open mystery' available to every human being.

The Old Testament

In the introduction we mentioned that the Trinitarian motif is already present in the Old Testament. It also seems clear that ancient mystery knowledge, knowledge of the highest divinity,

---

* *The Mystery of the Trinity and the Mission of the Spirit,* lecture of July 30, 1922.

also flowed into the content of the Old Testament. We cannot overlook the Trinitarian principle in the patriarchs and kings of the Old Testament.

Abraham is truly the father, the progenitor of his people. 'The lap of Abraham' is the place of final safety and happiness after death (as in the tale of the rich man and the poor Lazarus in Luke 16).

Abraham has one legitimate son: Isaac. Foreshadowing Christianity, he sacrifices his son. At the last moment the place of the son is taken by a ram.

The third patriarch is Jacob. His twin, Esau is removed from the line of inheritance, to make room for the more evolved spiritual stream of the line of Jacob. Jacob tricks his father to bless him rather than his brother; he sees the angels descending and ascending — Jacob's ladder — and is also the only one who says of himself that he has been 'face to face' with God. In the Old Testament this is an extraordinary statement (Gen.32:30), as normally the sight of God is held to be fatal.

The formula 'God of our fathers, the God of Abraham, Isaac and Jacob,' is typically Trinitarian. The three 'fathers' — with all their human traits — show the archetype of the Trinity at work.

The same is true of the first kings, Saul, David and Solomon. Saul is a powerful father figure, despite ending tragically. 'There was not a man among the people of Israel more handsome than he: from his shoulders upward he was taller than any of the people' (1Sam.9:2). Saul was the first in a long line of kings who lived about a thousand years after Abraham.

David follows him. He suffers persecution and great deprivation. The external events shaping Isaac's life are for David inner experiences and they foreshadow the life of Christ. In David's Psalm of 'forsakenness' (22), we can hear the words later spoken by Christ on the cross. The good shepherd is also a frequent topic in the Psalms of David (famously Psalm 23). Most clearly of all, the words God speaks during the baptism in the

Jordan: 'You are my son, today I have begotten you,' are words first spoken by David (Psalm 2:7).

Solomon is the third in the triad and an obvious representative of the Holy Spirit. His all-encompassing wisdom and clarity of judgment were legendary. Solomon's wisdom and insight built the Temple in Jerusalem. The Temple was then the 'body,' the dwelling for the highest divinity; much in the same sense as in the New Testament the Holy Spirit prepared the body of Jesus of Nazareth to be the dwelling of the Christ.

Shem, Ham and Japheth, sons of Noah, and the 'fathers' of the three main tribes after the great flood (Gen.9:18ff) are further examples of the Trinitarian principle, preceding the patriarchs Abraham, Isaac and Jacob, and the kings Saul, David and Solomon.

God in the Old Testament had the name Elohim. It actually means Gods. The name appears over a thousand times in the Old Testament and it is often translated in the plural. It would be an oversimplification to say that Elohim is a name for the Trinity, it is nevertheless remarkable that such a name is used in the Jewish monotheistic religion with its emphasis on the one God.

We find Elohim already in the first sentences of the Old Testament, 'Elohim created.' It is remarkable that the Hebrew *bara* (meaning 'he created') is singular, while the subject, Elohim, is plural. We can suppose that behind the singular is hidden the Trinity. Later we hear: 'Then God said, "Let us make man in our image, after our likeness",' (Gen.1:26). Who is speaking with whom here?

The story of the visitation of Abraham makes it even more apparent, showing frequent changes from singular to plural: 'And the LORD appeared to him by the oaks of Mamre ... He lifted up his eyes and looked, and behold three men stood in front of him.' One appeared, but Abraham saw three. However, he addresses them as one, but continues in the plural: 'My lord, if I have found favour in your [singular] sight ... Let water be brought and wash your [plural] feet, and rest yourselves ... that you may refresh yourselves ...' The story continues for a while in the plural, but then changes again: 'They said to him, "Where is Sarah your wife?" And he said, "She is in the tent." The LORD said, "I will surely return to you in the spring ...".' And then story returns to the plural: 'The men set out from there' (Gen.18:1–16).

Several more times before the end of the visitation (18:33) there is this enigmatic changing between singular and plural. It leaves us wondering. What does this mean? Was the writer perhaps being inconsistent? Or is it an indication of the mysterious nature of the Trinity?

In addition to the two elements we have looked at — the threefold figures of patriarchs and kings, and the subtle changes from singular to plural in the stories of the creation and of Abraham, another element is the many Old Testament texts which are threefold. The blessing of Aaron is a very significant example because in the Jewish tradition this threefold text also plays an important role.

> The LORD bless you and keep you:
> The LORD make his face to shine upon you, and be
> gracious to you:
> The LORD lift up his countenance upon you, and give
> you peace (Num.6:24–26).

In all the examples we have touched upon here, dogma plays no role; rather they reveal a living and dynamic presence of the Trinity, a divine reality, traceable as far back as the ancient mysteries.

If we look at the Trinitarian thoughts in the New Testament and its role in the development of Christianity, we will see similarities.

The New Testament

In the New Testament the idea and the reality of the Trinity lives and breathes like a living stream, and more clearly 'visibly' than in the Old Testament. The dogma of the Trinity is the later result of studies of New Testament texts; it is not stated explicitly in the New Testament. Let us to begin with take a look at three great events of Christ's life on earth: his baptism, transfiguration and his appearance after the resurrection.

During the baptism of Jesus in the Jordan the Trinity is present: Father, Son and Holy Spirit. Below Jesus stands in the Jordan already permeated by the Son, the Christ. The voice of the Father sounds from above, speaking about his Son, 'This is my beloved Son.' The Holy Spirit in the form of the dove, is the mediator.

During the transfiguration on the mountain the Trinity is just as clearly present: In Jesus, whose being has been permeated and transfigured by the presence of Christ in him; in the voice of the Father-God (again speaking of his Son) and in the Holy Spirit, who manifests his presence in the form of a luminescent cloud 'overshadowing' the event.

The 'overshadowing' of the Holy Spirit is also mentioned during the Annunciation (Luke 1:35): 'Holy Spirit will come upon you; the power of the Highest God will overshadow you, and the holy being to be born to you will be called Son of God.' Here again there is the Trinitarian aspect: the message of the Father about the Son, and the Spirit's mediating role in bringing it about.

A further testimony of the Trinity is the first appearance of the resurrected Christ to his disciples. Christ shows the disciples his wounds. He speaks to them of his Father: 'As the Father has sent me, so I send you.' And then he breathed on them and said, 'Receive the Holy Spirit!' (John 20:21f).

In a much more subtle way the Trinitarian element appears in the Book of Revelation. The appearance of the Son of Man

(Rev.1) is described with three times three characteristics. The rider on a white horse has three names (Rev.19). Another example is the vision of the throne. 'See, a throne stood in heaven and there was one seated on it. In his radiance he was like jasper and carnelian, and round the throne was a bow of colour which shone like an emerald' (Rev.4:2f). The throne, the One on the throne and a rainbow are present in the image. It is the being of the Father who is on the throne, but shortly after this we find the words: 'in the midst of the throne ... stood a Lamb' (Rev.5:6), showing an element of the Son in the One on the throne. The rainbow represents the all-embracing might of the Spirit, much as the throne represents the unshakeable ground and majesty of the Father.

In many other images of this kind we can discover representations of the divine Trinity. At the end of Matthew's Gospel, for instance, Christ sends his disciples on a mission: 'Go forth and be teachers of all peoples and baptize them in the name and with the power of the Father, and of the Son and of the Holy Spirit' (Mat.28:19).

The triad of names appears often in the St Paul's epistles: 'The grace of Jesus Christ the Lord, the love of God and the fellowship of the Holy Spirit be with you all' (2Cor.13:14). Others are in Romans 8:14–17, 15:15f, Second Corinthians 1:21f, Ephesians 3:14–17, 5:18–20, as well as in the First Letter of Peter (1:2).

Beyond these there is a plethora of similar word and image combinations throughout the New Testament. Two will be mentioned here in addition to the Prologue of the Gospel of John which was discussed earlier (p. 100).

In Luke 2 the angels sing:

> God be revealed in the heights
> and peace on earth
> to men of good will.

This example shows that the Trinity is hardly ever mentioned as a set formula, but in living images. John often brings it in a very subtle way: 'The Father showed HIS love for the world through this, that HE offered up HIS only Son. From now on, no one shall perish who fills himself with his power; indeed, he shall win a share of the life that is beyond time' (3:16). Some of the formulations in the Revelation are more obvious, like the oft-repeated words, 'who is and who was and who is coming.'

We encounter the mystery of the Trinity in the sequence of parables as well: in Luke 15 the three parables of the lost sheep, the lost coin and the lost son. The relationship to Christ is obvious in the first parable: *Christ*, the shepherd seeks the lost sheep until he finds it. In the third parable the *father* waits for the return of the son who was lost. The middle parable has the light as a motif: light has to be kindled to search for what has been lost. This is the light of the *Spirit*.

Many other examples could be cited showing the living relationship of the Trinity in human beings. It is an invitation to experience the power and presence of the Trinity in a living way rather than dogmatize the content. However, the dogma did save the knowledge from vanishing into oblivion when the possibilities of experience had been lost.

History and development of the dogma

Attempts to explain the mystery of the Trinity began in the second century. Attempts were made to safeguard the mystery against errors, misinterpretations and one-sided views in the search for the 'true faith.' In the course of many centuries various dogmas were formulated, which circumscribed the boundaries of the Christian faith.

It can seem quite extraordinary that despite the wide variety of opinions, despite political manoeuvring and attempts to explain and understand which were limited by their age, the formula that evolved contained the mystery of the Trinity. Even at that time no one understood it, and it was simply a matter of faith to Christian believers. It is not surprising really that it should have become a dogma. After all monotheism — the absolute oneness of God — was the foundation and how else, if not dogmatically, could the differentiations between Father, Son and Holy Spirit be explained?

The most varied cultural streams added their insights in the course of time: Platonism, Hellenism, Gnosis, early rabbinic Judaism and — possibly most significantly — the still hidden knowledge of the mystery schools which, though secret, still worked without revealing its origin.

At any rate, grave errors were avoided. One of them, later called modalistic monarchianism, said that the Son and the Spirit were 'masks' of the one God; Noetus for instance said that the Father himself suffered in Jesus and died in him. And while this view held on to the unity of the Trinity it failed to explain the differences. Dynamic monarchianism appeared in the third century; while it addressed the different aspects, it maintained that Christ was a subject of the monarch, his Father. A further variation came with adoptionism: Jesus was so human he could only be seen as the adopted son. The divinity of the Son was lost in this view. However, ignoring these variations would as a logical conclusion have ultimately led to tritheism.

We see that it was difficult if not impossible to think 'Three in One and One in Three' as a dynamic unity. This is why it became necessary to find a formulation to explain the inexplicable. This indeed happened during the great Church Councils in the fourth and fifth centuries.

Church history tells of two main opponents, both with unusually strong convictions. Beginning in AD 315 in Alexandria, Arius was the proponent of the one side. He denied the eternal being of Christ since there was, in his view, a time when Christ was not (namely before he was begotten by the Father). Arius maintained that Christ is *like* God and yet not *equal* to God. Athanasius on the other side took exception to the view. He firmly believed in the divine Sonship, and defended it to such a degree that complete non-differentiation was the result. In order to defend such a view, the equality of Father and Son became sameness, the only difference being that the Father was 'not conceived' while the Son was conceived. What this meant in its further implications was less clear.

Once again we can see that dynamic concepts were unavailable. While Athanasius quite rightly held the belief of the divine Sonship of Christ, he demanded total equality of Father and Son and thus denied any substantial difference.

Not surprisingly Arias commanded much respect and had many followers. His views were much easier to understand. And while in the year 325 the Council at Nicaea established the dogma of homoöusion (of one substance), and Arius was declared a heretic, it did not deter a large number of Christians, especially the Germanic tribes, to continue to follow Arius into the seventh century. Trinitarian dogma was too abstract for them.

However, this view easily led to an inadequate understanding of the being of Christ; Athanasius saw the truth more clearly, though he had not the means to clarify in depth.

The next problem was how to explain the divinity of the Holy Spirit. Another Church Council (Constantinople in 381) led to a further dogma, so that after four centuries the unity of the Trinity was firmly anchored in the Church.

One further step remained. The homoöusion of Athanasius had taken the Church very close to modalism (one God in three guises). It became necessary to conceptualize more clearly the meaning of 'Three in One and One in Three,' which had been an ongoing riddle and remained a mystery.

Tertullian had coined the term, *una substantia et tres persona*, one substance and three persons. The accepted version was formulated during the Church Council of Chalcedon in 451. *Substantia* became *essentia* or *natura* (Greek *physis)*: One *nature* and three *persons*.

In looking at the development of the dogma, we can see the train of thoughts and the nature of the difficulties. The truth of the Trinity was accepted, yet understanding remained sketchy. In addition, there was the dogma of the 'dual nature' of Christ; Christ is truly man and truly God. The *filioque* mentioned earlier led to the schism between East and West.

Many more attempts to understand, defend and explain followed in later centuries. The most outstanding theologians who sought a deeper understanding of the nature of the Trinity were Thomas of Aquinas, Master Eckhart and Nicholas of Cusa.

We are now left with the question: is the knowledge of the Trinity alive and well in Christianity? Has the dogma reduced it to a mere formula, used when making the sign of the cross or during baptisms for instance? Would it not be true to say that a living knowledge of the Trinity ceased altogether during recent centuries? It is indeed true that few attempts to rethink the issue have been made since the time of the Councils.

It is all the more important therefore to honour the fact that the dogma did at least save the truth of the Trinity from oblivion. It saved Christianity from simple monotheism (like Islam) and from becoming a three-god faith.

A renewed understanding of the Trinitarian mystery is now possible and is beginning. Anthroposophy and the renewal of the sacraments have opened the doors to new experiences and reflections. We will devote the last chapter of this book to the new knowledge given to the world through anthroposophy.

CHAPTER 6

Anthroposophy and the Trinity

Anthroposophy works in many areas of science and culture, endowing each with new insights and impulses. Much information is available to those wanting to know more.

With Rudolf Steiner and anthroposophy, new and decisive insights into the mystery of the Trinity as a living reality became available; a new light was shed on Christianity and on all the religions.

The first and second part of this book relied on and benefited greatly from Rudolf Steiner's insights.

Basic principles

Anthroposophy fully supports the Christian understanding of the Trinity. Throughout his work Rudolf Steiner mentions the Trinity not only in relation to the dogma and its consequences but also in detailed descriptions of the Trinitarian life and work.

We briefly quoted Rudolf Steiner in the previous chapter. Here is a more extensive extract.

> The Father is the unbegotten begetter who places the Son into the physical world. But at the same time the Father uses the Holy Spirit in order to tell humanity that in the spirit, the supersensible is comprehensible, even if this spirit is itself not perceptible ...

At the time the message of the Holy Spirit and his appearance at the baptism was initiated through the Father. And when Christ sent the Holy Spirit to his disciples — this imparting occurred through Christ, through the Son. For this reason it was an ancient dogma that the Father is the unbegotten begetter, that the Son is the one begotten by the Father, and that the Holy Spirit is the one imparted to humanity by the Father and the Son. This is not some kind of arbitrarily asserted dogma but rather the wisdom of initiation living in the earliest Christian centuries; only later was it covered over and buried along with the teachings concerning the Trichotomy and the Trinity.

The divine principle working as Christianity within evolving humanity cannot be understood without the Trinity. If, in place of the Trinity, some other teaching concerning God were to enter, then basically speaking it would not be a fully Christian teaching. One must understand the Father, the Son, and the Holy Spirit if one would understand the teaching concerning God concretely and in a genuine way.[*]

In a later lecture Rudolf Steiner adds:

The idea of the Trinity of the Father God, of the Son God, and God of the Holy Spirit is not a cleverly thought-out formula. It is something deeply united with the entire evolution of the cosmos. When we bring Christ himself as the Resurrected One to life within us, then our knowledge of the Trinity is not dead but alive, for Christ is the bringer of the Holy Spirit.[†]

[*] *The Mystery of the Trinity and the Mission of the Spirit,* lecture of July 30, 1922.
[†] As above, lecture of August 27, 1922.

A third passage comes from a lecture given to workers at the Goetheanum.

> The people of past times thus said the divine principle came to revelation in three ways. You see, they might have said: there is a god of nature, a god of will, and a god of spirit, where the will is hallowed again and made spiritual. They actually did say this, for the old words meant just that. 'Father' was something connected with the origins of the physical world, a natural principle. In the languages we have now, the significance of these words has been lost. But those people of old would add something when they said there is a god of nature, the Father, a god of will, the Son, and a god of spirit, the Holy Ghost who heals all that has grown sick because of the will. They would add: 'These three are one.' Their most important statement, their greatest conviction therefore was this: 'The divine has three forms, but these three are one.'
>
> Something else they would say was: 'If you look at a human being, you see a big difference from the natural world. If you look at a stone, what is active in it? The Father. If you look at a plant, what is active in it? The Father God. If you look at the human being as a physical human being, what is active in it? The Father God. However, if you look at the human being as soul, in his will, what is active in this? The Son God. And if you consider the future of humanity, how it shall be one day when all shall be healthy again in the will — that is where the Spirit God is at work.' All three gods, they would say, are active in the human being. There are three gods or divine forms; but they are one, and they also work as one in the human being.
>
> That was the original Christians' belief.*

* From *Beetroot to Buddhism*, lecture of March 19, 1924.

We have here three characteristic examples of the basic principles of anthroposophy, showing us how strongly the reality of the Trinity is linked to the anthroposophical worldview. It will become ever clearer when we now consider various topics in greater detail.

Rudolf Steiner's theory of knowledge

It is important for us to keep in mind that anthroposophy does not merely speak to us of the Trinity in many and varied ways but also that it shows ways and means to nurture the actual experience of the Trinity at work in us. This is most apparent in the fact that the anthroposophical theory of knowledge is three-fold in nature. The Trinitarian principle permeates the entire creation, and observation of the world leads to its rediscovery. We already considered this when we looked at the threefold nature of plants.

The threefold approach in the theory of knowledge, which Rudolf Steiner developed in the 1890s, is as follows. The human being meets the world initially through a multitude of sense perceptions. These would remain merely sense perceptions or percepts if we did not begin to think about them, and by thinking about them reach insights and knowledge. So we have two points of departure: percepts and concepts. It is not difficult to discover the Father principle in the former and the Spirit principle in the latter, since our perceptions reveal the given world, a world that *is*. When we begin to think we are spiritually active participants in the emergence of our thoughts.

A third element has to join for understanding to emerge: we need a link between perception and thinking, to give us a sense of the reality in the world. Thinking and perception have to be 'married.' And that is the principle of the Son in us. The full reality of anything 'given,' is revealed to us only by means of the link between perceiving and thinking.

It is important to add that what we understand through our efforts, connecting percepts and concepts, and see as order, form and purpose only reveals these aspects because order, form and purpose are inherent in the world. There is no division, but a unity of substance, purpose and manifestation.

For instance in a plant we have the *substantial nature* of the plant in its matter. Secondly there is an ordered unity and form which reveals the *idea* of the plant. Thirdly there is the weaving together of idea and substance in the growth and decay of a particular manifestation of the plant. The reality of the plant is a working of the three elements in unity.

Each element — substance, idea (purpose and form), and growth/decay is quite different from the others. In our consciousness they appear differently — through perception and thinking — and must be brought together. This example shows the Trinitarian principle at work. It is the basic method within the process of cognition itself.

Threefold unity

It is part of the anthroposophical view of the world and the human being to see the Trinitarian principle at work in threefold ways.

We mentioned the plant as a visible example several times. The triune of body, soul and spirit is of the utmost importance. The Trinity of Father-God, Son-God and Spirit-God is mirrored in the triune of body (Father), soul (Son) and spirit (Holy Spirit). We again see three separate entities working in unison. Each one of these parts is again a working harmony of three. The body is a unity of the nerve-sense system, the rhythmic system (blood circulation and breathing), and the metabolic-limb system. The soul lives within a threesome of soul-activities of thinking, feeling and will. And Rudolf Steiner points out in his book *Theosophy*, the spirit will in future unfold three capacities of spirit-self, life-spirit and spirit-endowed humanity.

Every one of these triunes mirrors the divine Trinity, which is their uniting factor. They are always working in unison and not as separate entities.

This constitutional, — physiological, psychological and spiritual — threefold unity of human beings has its equivalent in the social sphere. After the First World War Rudolf Steiner pointed out with great intensity how important it is to acknowledge and nurture fundamental threefold principles within social life and social organizations.

In many lectures and from various angles he showed the need for a restructuring of social life into three parts working in unity. The sphere of culture and art, the legal sphere, and the economic sphere.

He pointed out that these three spheres were related to the three great ideals of the French Revolution — liberty, equality and fraternity. These could not come to bear because there was no clarity about their respective relevance. Only if they are applied in the right context and only if the three spheres of activity are distinguished, will a healthy and balanced social life be possible.

Liberty reigns in the cultural sphere which has to be completely free.

Equality is essential in the legal sphere.

Fraternity is the guiding principle of the economic sphere which functions through cooperation and brotherliness.

We can only point out a few basic thoughts here. But we can see the Trinitarian principle clearly at work as a fundamental threefold idea, which distinguishes the spheres and works together.

The Trinity and evil

A further field of anthroposophical observations showing the Trinitarian principle is in the area of evil. The forces of evil approach human beings from two sides. On the one side is the self-aggrandizement, arrogance and egotism, and on the other the tendency to rigidity and materialism. Such tendencies can be tracked in many forms and on many levels which lead human beings into one-sidedness while taking them away from striving for the good. It shows itself in one-sided idealism or materialism — the flight from the earth's realities on the one side, or addiction to the lures of earthly temptations on the other.

Earlier in the book we mentioned the role of the Holy Spirit, whose presence in us helps us to overcome one-sidedness and strengthens the capacities of the middle ground. The middle path leads between flight and addiction, leads us to strive for acceptance of the earth and to work in it out of awareness of the spiritual. And to seek the spiritual not out of selfish desire, but to find the strength for our task on earth.

The one-sidedness of the forces of evil in appear on the soul-level for instance as greed or wastefulness (the middle path is the right relationship to money), as timidity or recklessness (the middle is courage), as depression or euphoria (the middle is equanimity), as pessimism or optimism, and so on. In the body the forces of evil appear, for instance, as illnesses in the extremes of fever or shivers, as anorexia or gluttony, as sclerosis or as dissolving tendencies. The healthy balance whether of soul or of body always lies in the middle.

These examples show why Rudolf Steiner speaks of two polarizing forces of evil, of two adversaries called Lucifer and Ahriman. In the Bible they are called Satan and the devil, or the snake and the dragon, in the book of Job their names are Leviathan and Behemoth. In a well known picture by Albrecht Dürer, *The Knight, the Devil and Death,* the human being is accompanied by the two adversaries; death is here the representative of Ahriman.

It can move us deeply that the Trinitarian principle also appears in human life as a demonic mirror image to the divine Trinity. Christ, the Son is always the true mediator, as much as the human middle ground is the path to health giving choice.

Father, Son and Holy Spirit in human life

The very deep the relationship between human destiny and the Trinity becomes apparent when we consider the following two examples. Anthroposophical pedagogy rests on the knowledge that human development proceeds through three different spheres of world-experience, individual self-experience and the experience of self in and with the world in the first twenty-one years.

These three seven-year periods are linked to the Trinity. Most obviously the first seven years mirror the Father. Not only is the child completely dependent on sustenance and care, it learns by imitation, and the development of the body is prominent. Even religion at that age is something physical, according to Rudolf Steiner. Abstract thinking has little relevance, for the child absorbs and 'incorporates' the world through its sense organs, hearing, feeling, tasting, seeing and rhythmical movement.

Religion is its nature. The child is naturally devoted, believing and open to everything around it. While the child does not 'think' religion, it is naturally religious, and, apart from graces and evening prayers, church-going is neither called for nor necessary. Everything in the child's environment including the daily rhythm should be structured in such a way that it can be absorbed without harm by its trusting and open nature. Young children do not have personal boundaries and are unable to close off the influences of their environment.

The situation changes dramatically after the fourteenth year. Now the youngster's drive is for independence and inner freedom, often at the price of peace at home. High ideals and goals come into view. While in the first seven-year period we see the nature of the Father-God predominating, we now see the Spirit-God at work.

Between these two seven-year periods are the years from seven to fourteen, a time when the soul-forces of thinking, feeling and will develop. Their health depends very much on the nurture of the individuating faculties: the sense for harmony and beauty in the world, love of being alive and a beginning of understanding that life itself is meaningful. These are the Christ-years in the evolving human being and they need careful nurture and healthy engagement so that in the next phase they can be grasped in inner freedom and with strength of purpose.

The inner relationship with the life of a plant is visible during these first three seven-year periods. The first seven years 'root' the child to the earth. Much can be done during these years to nurture the feeling of belonging to the earth and its communities. In the second seven-year period faculties unfold and after that a flowering and first 'fruiting' becomes obvious. Each stage lays the foundations for the next.

The second motif we will take up here is the threefold inner meeting of human beings with the Trinity. The first meeting happens every night when we sleep. We meet our angel, the genius of our life, and through the meeting with the angel shines the light of the Spirit-God. Rudolf Steiner spoke about this in 1917.

> We now come to the first meeting of which we have to speak. When does it take place? It takes place quite simply in normal sleep, on almost every occasion, between sleeping and waking. With simple country people, who are nearer to the life of nature, and who go to bed with the setting sun and get up at sunrise, this meeting takes place in the middle of their sleeping time, which as a rule is the middle of the night. With people who have detached themselves from their connections with nature, this is not so much the case. But this depends on man's free will. A man of modern culture can regulate his life as he pleases, and though this fact is bound to affect his life, still he can regulate it as he likes, within certain limits. None the less he too can experience in the middle of a

long sleep, what may be called an inner union with the Spirit-Self — that is, with the Spiritual qualities from which the Spirit-Self will be extracted; he can have a meeting with his genius. Thus this meeting with one's genius takes place every night, that is, during every period of sleep — though this must not be taken too literally. This meeting is important for man. For all the feelings that gladden the soul with respect to its connection with the Spiritual world proceed from this meeting with one's genius during sleep. The feeling, which we may have in our waking state, of our connection with the Spiritual world, is an after-effect of this meeting with our genius. That is the first meeting with the higher world; and it may be said that most people are at first unconscious of it, though they will become more and more conscious the more they realise its after-effects by refining their waking conscious life, through absorbing the ideas and conceptions of Spiritual Science, until their souls become refined enough to observe carefully these after-effects. It all depends on whether the soul is refined enough, sufficiently acquainted with its inner life, to be able to observe these. This meeting with the genius is brought to the consciousness of every man in some form or other; but the materialistic surroundings of the present day which fill the mind with ideas coming from the materialistic view of the world and especially the life of today, permeated as it is by materialistic opinions, prevent the soul from paying attention to what comes as the result of the meeting. As people gradually fill their minds with more Spiritual ideas than those set forth by materialism, the perception of the nightly meeting with the genius will become more and more self-evident to them.*

* *Cosmic and Human Metamorphoses,* lecture of February 20, 1917.

A second meeting occurs once a year during the night at Christmas. During that time, though it normally remains unconscious, every human soul meets Christ through the intercession of an archangel. Some of the magic of Christmas is related to this meeting. Rudolf Steiner describes this.

The second meeting of which we now have to speak is higher. From the indications already given it may be gathered that the first meeting with the genius is in connection with the course of the day. If we had not, through modern civilisation, become free to adjust our lives according to our own convenience, this meeting would take place at the hour of midnight. A man would meet his genius every night at midnight. But on account of man's exercise of free will the time of this meeting has become movable; the hour when the ego meets the genius is now not fixed. The second meeting is however not so movable; for that which is more connected with the astral body and etheric body is not so apt to get out of its place in the cosmic order. That which is connected with the ego and the physical body is very greatly displaced in present-day man. The second meeting is already more in connection with the great macro-cosmic order. Even as the first meeting is connected with the course of the day, the second meeting is connected with the course of the year. I must here call attention to various things I have already indicated in this connection from another point of view. The life of man in its entirety does not run its course quite evenly through the year. When the sun develops its greatest heat, man is much more dependent upon his own physical life and the physical life around him than in the winter when, in a sense, he has to struggle with the external phenomena of the elements, and is more thrown back on himself; but then his Spiritual nature is more freed, and he is more in

connection with the Spiritual world — both his own and
that of the earth — with the whole Spiritual environment. Thus the peculiar sentiment we connect with the
Mystery of Christmas and with its Festival is by no
means arbitrary, but hangs together with the fixing of the
Festival of Christmas. At that time in winter which is
appointed for the Festival, man, as does indeed the
whole earth, gives himself up to the Spirit. He then
passes, as it were, through a realm in which the Spirit is
near him. The consequence is that at about Christmas-
time and on to our present New Year, man goes through
a meeting of his astral body with the Life-Spirit, in the
same way as he goes through the first meeting, that of
his ego with the Spirit-Self. Upon this meeting with the
Life-Spirit depends the nearness of Christ Jesus. For
Christ Jesus reveals Himself through the Life-Spirit. He
reveals Himself through a being of the Realm of the
Archangels. He is, of course, an immeasurably higher
Being than they, but that is not the point with which we
are concerned at the moment; what we have to consider
is that He reveals Himself through a Being of the order of
the Archangeloi. Thus through this meeting we draw
specially near to Christ Jesus at the present stage of
development — which has existed since the Mystery of
Golgotha — and in a certain respect we may call the
meeting with the Life-Spirit: the meeting with Christ
Jesus in the very depths of our soul. Now when a man
either through developing Spiritual consciousness in the
domain of religious meditation or exercises, or, to supple-
ment these, has accepted the concepts and ideas of
Spiritual Science, when he has thus deepened and spiri-
tualised his life of impression and feeling, then, just as he
can experience in his waking life the after-effects of the
meeting with his Spirit-Self, so he will also experience
the after-effects of the meeting with the Life-Spirit, or

Christ. It is actually a fact, my dear friends, that in the time following immediately on Christmas and up to Easter the conditions are particularly favourable for bringing to a man's consciousness this meeting with Christ Jesus. In a profound sense and this should not be blotted out by the abstract materialistic culture of today — the season of Christmas is connected with processes taking place in the earth; for man, together with the earth, takes part in the Christmas changes in the earth. The season of Easter is determined by processes in the heavens. Easter Sunday is fixed for the first Sunday after the first full-moon after the Vernal Equinox. Thus, whereas Christmas is fixed by the conditions of the earth, Easter is determined from above. Just as we, through all that has just been described, are connected with the conditions of the earth, so are we connected, through what I shall now describe, with the conditions of the heavens — with the great Cosmic conditions. For Easter is that season in the concrete course of the year, in which all that is aroused in us by the meeting with Christ at Christmas, really unites itself with our physical earth manhood. The great Mystery that now brings home to man the Mystery of Golgotha at the Easter Season — the Good Friday Mystery — signifies among other things, that the Christ, who, as it were, has been moving beside us, at this season comes still closer to us. Indeed, roughly speaking, in a sense He disappears into us and permeates us, so that He can remain with us during the season that follows the Mystery of Golgotha — the season of summer — during which, in the ancient Mysteries, men tried to unite themselves to John in a way not possible after the Mystery Of Golgotha.*

* *Cosmic and Human Metamorphoses,* lecture of February 20, 1917.

The third meeting happens only once in a lifetime, around the age of thirty. It is a meeting with the Father-God and is essentially an inner experience of death.

Just as we can speak of the second as a meeting with Christ Jesus, so can we speak of the third as a meeting with the Father-Principle, with the Father, with that which lies at the foundation of the world, and which we experience when we have the right feeling for what the various religions mean by 'the Father.' This meeting is of such a nature that it reveals our intimate connection with the Macrocosm, with the Divine-Spiritual Universe. The daily course of universal processes, of world processes, includes our meeting with our genius: the yearly course includes our meeting with Christ Jesus: and the course of a whole human life, of this human life of ours, my dear friends — which can normally be described as the patriarchal life of seventy years — includes the meeting with the Father-Principle. For a certain time, our physical earth-life is prepared — and rightly so — by education — at the present day to a great extent unconsciously, yet it is prepared; and most people experience unconsciously, between the ages of twenty-eight and forty-two — and though unconsciously, yet fully appreciated in the intimate depths of the soul — the meeting with the Father-Principle. The after-effects of this may extend into later life, if we develop sufficiently fine perceptions to note that which thus comes into our life from within ourselves, as the after-effects of our meeting with the Father-Principle. During a certain period of our life — the period of preparation — education ought, in the many different ways this can be done, to make the meeting with the Father-Principle as profound an experience as possible. One way is to arouse in a man, during his years of education, a strong feeling of the glory of the world, of its greatness, and of the sublimity of the world-processes. We are withholding a great deal from the growing boy and girl if we fail to draw their attention to all the revelations of beauty and greatness in the world, for then, instead of having a devoted reverence and respect for these, they may pass them by unobserved. If we fill the minds of the young with thoughts connecting the feelings of their hearts with the beauty and greatness of the world, we are then preparing them for the right meeting with the Father-Principle.*

These two examples of anthroposophical thinking may serve to highlight the real work of the Trinity in human development. Similar principles can be found in many other areas of anthroposophical research. They show how strongly our existence is influenced, carried and nurtured by the Trinitarian principle.

Inasmuch as that the same is true in nature, we will dedicate the final chapter to further explorations into nature.

The Trinity in nature

We have already mentioned Trinitarian principles at work in nature in plants and in the human being. Angelus Silesius speaks about the nature of the Trinity in this poem:

> The Trinity of God
> Is shown in every plant
> Where sulphur, salt and mercury
> Three manifest as one.

The poem links the Trinity with alchemical processes, which played a prominent role in the Middle Ages. Sulphur, salt and mercury are processes necessary for the growth of

---

* *Cosmic and Human Metamorphoses,* lecture of February 20, 1917.

plants. The salt process is needed for the formation of root systems, to loosen the hardness of the soil and for the absorption of nutrients. The sulphur process is related to light and aids the formation of flowers and dissolving matter into lightness. The mercury process supports the plant's growth between root and flower. The plant is placed between the polarities of earth and light, between heaven and earth, between light and darkness. It uses the salt and sulphur processes and the mediating mercury process to develop its nature between these two contrasts.

The same principle applies to other realms in nature. The three kingdoms — mineral, plant and animal — find their reflection on a higher level in the human being. The aggregate states of solid, liquid and gas also reflect this.

An interesting threefold principle is apparent in the world of insects. Butterflies and beetles form a polarity between which the bees form a middle. The earth as a whole shows a threefold state with the frozen polar regions and the equatorial region as polarities and the temperate zones as balancing intermediary. The temperate zone in turn reflects the pattern in the polarities of summer and winter, and spring and autumn holding the balance.

Everywhere in the world, wherever we look, we can find the creative and life-bearing principle of the Trinity at work. It does not have to remain a Church dogma. With the help of anthroposophy we can raise our awareness to the world-creating principle of the Trinity.

Based on the above we will see how this can be a help in religious experience.

CHAPTER 7

Renewed Religion
in the Light of the Trinity

In this final chapter we will look at Christian religious life within The Christian Community. Some of the motifs have already been touched upon in previous chapters, as our aim in the first part of the book was to show possibilities of experiencing Father, Son and Holy Spirit with our modern consciousness and to open up our religious striving; The Christian Community exists to make create such possibilities.

The main task will be to show how much the centre of religious life, the seven sacraments, is permeated by the Trinity.

Fundamentals

The sign of the cross in the old Mass is accompanied by the words, 'In the name of the Father, the Son and the Holy Spirit.'

In a classical reformulation the Act of Consecration of Man, the renewed form of the Eucharist, has these words as three signs of the cross are made:

> The Father-God be in us
> The Son-God create in us
> The Spirit-God enlighten us.

A more concise and exact description of the Trinity is hardly possible. It is a progression from the old set formula to a wording which holds greater depth and substance.

Further enrichment comes from the Trinity Epistle, spoken at the beginning and end of the Act of Consecration at times when there is no particular festival. This Epistle speaks of the profound relationship between the Trinity and human beings: that our substance and being is the Father's substance and being; that our essence and life flows forth from the Son's creative life; that our beholding and knowing be graciously received into the light of the Spirit

The first and second sentences refer to the reality of our existence, our being and our life, while the third expresses hope that our beholding and knowing be 'graciously received,' which is not a given fact but something we have to aspire to in our daily life. In the realm of the Spirit we have to be and become consciously and knowingly active and from there transform our relationship to the Father and the Son.

Baptism

Making the sign of the cross has always accompanied the baptism, as Christ instructed his disciples to 'baptize ... in the name and with the power of the Father, and of the Son and of the Holy Spirit' (Matt.28:19).

The Christian Community has been accused of omitting these words. And indeed they are not used as such. But Christ could hardly have meant a formula to be used when he told us to baptize in the name of the Trinity.

The Sacrament of Baptism has been renewed and strengthened in substance and essence. Even if the formulaic words are not used, the Trinity is addressed and present during baptism. Three crosses signify that the person to be baptized is now placed into the world substance of the Father, into the word-stream of Christ, and into the shining light of the Spirit.

Here again we have descriptive and meaningful words in place of the old formula. We have already become familiar with the world-substance of the Father and the enlightening power of the Spirit. 'The word-stream of Christ' is a new element. It echoes the Gospel of John where the Son is the Logos, the Word. It also expresses how the Godhead, through the Son, relates to humankind. If we speak with someone, we hope to be heard and understood. In the 'Word,' in the being of Christ, lives the divine gift of the Father's promise to be with us and his hope to be heard by us. Into this divine hope the child is baptized.

The entire Sacrament of Baptism is founded on the knowledge of the Trinity. In addition to water salt and ash are used. The child is touched with the sign of the cross on the forehead with water, on the chin with water and salt and on the breast with water, salt and ash. Later in life, in the Act of Consecration of Man, the sign of the cross is made over the same locations, signifying our relationship with the Trinity.

The course of the year in the light of the Trinity

The Christian festivals in the course of the year bear the character of the Trinity.

— Advent, Christmas, Epiphany are festivals of the Father.
— Lent, Easter and Ascension are festivals of the Son.
— Whitsun, St John's Tide and Michaelmas are festivals of the Holy Spirit.

In addition to those three threefold festivals periods are four in-between periods. Between Whitsun and St John's Tide, between St John's Tide and Michaelmas, between Michaelmas and between Epiphany and Lent.

In the three times three festivals we can experience the course of the year as a living revelation of the Trinity. Looking in more detail, within each group of festivals each of the three persons can be found working within the overall dominance of one. So for instance, in the three festivals of the Father we see:

Advent: the Father
Christmas: the Son
Epiphany: the Spirit

A similar pattern can be found in the other festivals.

Christmas is — in the Father festival group — the festival of the birth of his Son on earth. The Son works out of the Father in the Father. The Son appears at Christmas in the aura of the Father, and the Father works together with the Son, while during Advent the Fatherly being is almost entirely in the foreground.

The Easter festival is a celebration entirely for the Son, the Sonship of the Son. Unlike at Christmas — the celebration of the birth and his entry into the world of time and space — at Easter we celebrate the creative deed of overcoming time and space with death and resurrection. This is truly the realm of the Son.

In a similar way we might look at the life and meaning of every festival in terms of the threefold presence of the Trinity at work in it.

Celebrated in such a way, the journey through the Christian festivals in the cycle of the year can bring us closer to the divine Trinity. It is not a matter of dogma; rather it is life in harmony with the moods of the seasons and the festivals that allows our relationship with the divine powers. The mood at Lent and Easter is completely different from the mood of Advent and Christmas. It is up to us to become aware of these moods and to have an inkling of the deep significance of these festivals. The Christian year itself leads us into a differentiated and luminous experience of the Trinity.

The Epistles

The Act of Consecration of Man derives its special fullness of colour to a large degree from the seasonal prayers, the Epistles. They are spoken at the beginning and the end of the service and their wording highlights the essence and nature of each festival, creating ever new and varied insights.

Let us look first at some of the words in relation to the Father. At Advent we hear of 'the silent world around us' as an inner experience within which something of the Father's strength and grounding stillness can meet us. Included in the Epistle is also the 'divine might' of the Father-God, apparent in the sun and in the 'bow of colour, spanning the sky.' They fade into the twilight, while inner colourfulness and sunshine proclaim the birth on earth of the living Word of the Father.

Every time we manage to allow peace to dwell in our soul we enter into the mood of Advent; our soul touches the quiet stillness of the Father's being, which is at the same time full of creative movement. In the quiet stillness in us, the future ripens, the coming of something new, waiting to be born. Once the external world fades into twilight, a new world will be born from the Father Ground.

The inner experience of 'the fatherly Ground of the World' and 'the Father-Ground of all existence' is deepened in St John's Tide through the words: 'all-blessing, all-wielding.' Perhaps 'all-blessing' best describes the most profound inward beholding of the Father. He lives in completeness of being, himself unmoved, yet all-creating in the birth of a new world, blessing and permeating all with his peace.

The wording of the Epistles of the Son is equally descriptive of his nature. 'The health-bringing power of the Christ' is mentioned already in the creed. During Advent our hearts can feel his healing power 'quickening in the womb of the world.' At Christmas this feeling is elevated to inner beholding of Christ 'the bringer of healing' to earthly man' and to feeling the 'healing word' of the Creator. The motif changes at Easter when we hear the words of his 'healing might,' which, — through the power of the Risen-One — works right into the beating of our heart as well as healing our innermost self. And at St John's Tide the words reach a greater height when he is named 'Saviour of mankind needy of healing.'

We become increasingly aware that the word 'Saviour' is intimately linked with healing:

— healing quickens (germinates) in the womb of the world,
— the 'creative healing Word' and the 'bringer of healing' at Christmas
— his healing might reaches into the beat of our heart and heals our innermost self in the darkness of the soul at Easter.
— mankind needy of healing feels the presence of Christ at St John's Tide.

The words hold the seeds for a new theology. It is important to note that the ritual texts point to the very real stream of life-strength flowing through the world during the times of the Christian festivals.

We will briefly touch upon another motif. It may seem unusual for traditional Christians to hear, in the St John's epistle, the words the 'sun of Christ,' for its heathen connotation. While the term has lost much of its original meaning in the course of time, some remnants have been preserved in poetry or songs. In the Old Testament Malachi (4:2) speaks of 'the sun of righteousness.'

The cosmic splendour of Christ — the universal sun-being — is described by Matthew in the Transfiguration on the mountain: 'And he was transformed before them. His countenance shone like the sun' (17:2). In the Apocalypse the face of the Son of Man 'shone like the sun in its full power' (Rev.1:16).

The cosmic, sunlike being of Christ, of which we spoke previously (The Cosmic Christ, p. 47) is also present in the Epistles. Beginning with Advent, the 'eternal, divine wielding word' — the Son — has been 'born of light.' During Epiphany we hear the words: 'the world's light in the star of grace,' 'Christ star,' 'the gracious appearance of the world's light,' and 'the warm shining of divine salvation.' The sun-being of Christ comes into full view in all the images of the Epistle of St John's Tide.

At Easter the light-motif is already radiantly present. It shows that the earth itself is being transformed into a being of light. Through the resurrection of Christ it is transformed into 'spirit-radiant power of the sun.' In his light can be born anew what otherwise will languish in 'the chains of death.' The divine light can shine again in and from the human 'I.' It is not coincidental that in Mark 16 we meet the image of the sun rising out of darkness and that the two women, as they go to the grave on Easter Sunday are accompanied by the rising sun — images with deep meaning and power.

St John's Tide finally acquaints us with the 'sun of Christ,' 'our deliverer.' Christ is called upon as the 'sun-spirit' who enters the human realm, whose light is grace, is 'the radiant grace of light.' He is the bringer and the creator of light, who endows our senses with his 'light's fullness of love' so that we can experience and fill our souls with his healing grace.

Christ, the Healer, is a fundamental Christian motif. The words 'Christ, the sun-spirit' resurrect for Christianity the deep feeling human beings had in the distant past. They describe in the most profound sense of relationship human beings can have with the divine world, whether in Christianity or outside it: the sense that God is not distant, but is with us, like the sun, warming us and giving light and life in abundance. When Christ came to earth these feelings were internalized and not expressed, remaining in the background as the religious life of Christians turned inward. Now it is time to rekindle the experience of the cosmic dimensions of the Son of God.

And thus Christ now stands before us in the Epistles as the 'Healer' as well as the sun-spirit.

— The Word, the creative power of the sun-spirit, the One
    born from light (Advent).
— At Epiphany the grace-bestowing power is experienced as '
    'the light of grace.'
— At Easter this becomes the help and strength to be reborn,
    when the earth shines anew in the light of his 'spirit-radi-
    ant power of the sun.'
— And finally at St John's Tide 'the sun of Christ' is revealed.

These examples may show how multifaceted our knowledge and experience of the Trinity can become in the course of the year, when we follow the Christian year through the words of the Epistles. What was dogmatic tradition can become an experience full of life and colour.

The words describing the Spirit-God are fewer. This may be because the wonder of the images and the wording in the renewed ritual is already a testament of the healing Spirit-light. In the sacraments the Holy Spirit, his 'life shining with spirit,' works into our lives, permeating and renewing all.

At Whitsun, however, something is said about the Spirit. The healing Spirit is called the 'world-physician' who heals the 'sickness of the souls', and 'the infirmities of mankind.' This adds a further dimension to the healing power of Christ mentioned earlier. Christ's healing power was sacrificed and offered as stream of life to humankind and to the earth. He gave his body and his blood, so that they would become the body and the blood of human beings.

The healing power of the Spirit works in human consciousness, as we mentioned earlier. Human beings are ill and weak due to the denial of their own spirituality, which leads to lamed and darkened consciousness, to dependency on the senses, to fascination with illusions, and to errors of judgment.

Into the darkness of human spirituality the light of spiritual-ized thinking must fall and remove the powers of darkness. 'The healing light of grace,' the light of the Spirit will shine into the 'earth-night,' 'into sense-darkness,' as it says in the Christmas Epistle. Healing begins within the innermost self of the human being.

Both processes work in unison: from the side of the Son and from the side of the Holy Spirit. The Spirit has something of the role of a doctor, who has to diagnose the illness and then to make the patient aware of the cause so that healing can begin. The healing medicines are essential to allow the life processes to work healthily, and at times even a blood-transfusion may be needed.

In the same sense the 'world-physician' knows the 'diagno-sis of the world's illnesses' and shows both the process causing the illness as well as the treatment needed. Healing depends on our active engagement with healing processes, and here the con-sciousness for the need of healing is the first and most important step to take. We can call on the healing powers of Christ, which he offers through the offering of his life-substances.

The Trinity and the sacraments

All sacraments have their origin in the life and offering of Christ himself. From them flows a sevenfold stream of offering sub-stances into the earth and into humankind. In that sense the seven sacraments are a sevenfold manifestation of the Son and his work on earth. The manifold aspects of the Trinity are at also work within the sacraments — the realm of the Son — similar to the way they work in the festivals.

Baptism is a thoroughly Trinitarian sacrament. Though essen-tially based on the life of the Son, it is also the sacrament most strongly related to the Father. Babies are unconscious of their own self and are entirely dependent on the nurture and protec-tion of their parents or carers — they are 'grounded' in them.

Confirmation is the sacrament of the Spirit (see also our consideration of the seven-year periods, p. 128) The time of Confirmation is the time to forge a conscious relationship with the Son, something that is developmentally not possible before the fourteenth year.

The *Ordination* into the priesthood also demands a steady and conscious deepening of the relationship with the Christ, and relates the human being to the Spirit-God.

The *Act of Consecration of Man* is a sacrament celebrated daily, either at the altar or alone by the priest. It is very much a Christ-centred sacrament. It requires our faithfulness and mindful presence, since it renews and upholds, on a daily basis, the offering of the body and the blood of Christ for us.

Sacramental Consultation is an opportunity for an individual to consciously realign themselves to their aims and destiny. It is permeated by the Spirit-God.

In the sacrament of *Marriage* the most important element is faithfulness and care, directed towards forming a 'community of life.' This evolving 'body' is the actual substance addressed in the sacrament of marriage. The introductory words, which refer to Christ's as the one who 'transmuted work of earth into work of spirit in his own deed of sacrifice,' are singularly important and unique and relate the partners to the transcending, transforming power of Christ.

The *Last Anointing* stands at the end of life and takes us back to the realm of the Father who receives us back into his world.

Here again the working together of the Trinity can be seen in a wonderful way. The creative working of the Son takes into itself that of the Father and of the Spirit, transforms, intensifies and concentrates them. The Son bows to the Father, raises himself to the Spirit, taking the human being with him in these gestures. The Father gives himself to the Son and through him is transformed into love for humanity; the Father gives strength and substance to the light of the Spirit-God. The Spirit's light enlightens the world of the Father with clarity, beauty and grace, with infinite richness of form and possibilities. He takes the substance of Christ's offering and lifts it into the eternity of spirit existence. The inner working and life of the Trinity opens to our beholding hearts.

The working of the Trinity can be seen in the parts of the Act of Consecration of Man. The service begins by turning to Christ, with a prayer for the presence of his 'pure life' as we hear his words speaking to us through the reading of the *Gospels*. Hearing from the life of Christ gives us the strength to make an offering of our feeling, thinking and will to the Father. The Father is addressed to this end at the beginning of the *Offering*. Soon thereafter we turn again to the Christ, since our offering is too weak, and needs the help of Christ's sacrifice. And so the second part of the Offering turns again to the being of Christ. He completes what we lack.

Let us imagine the process vividly: From the pure life of Christ a steam flows through the Gospel and into our hearts. In answer our will is engaged to devote ourselves in offering to the lofty world of the Father. It is but a mere wisp of breath which goes to the Father. When it is supplemented by Christ's sacrificial deed, it becomes a cloud, or even fire, of offering.

The *Transubstantiation* opens with us turning once more to the Father-God. Now that our offering has united with Christ, our offering is also a Christ-offering. The priest kneels during the middle part of the Transubstantiation, during the dialogue between the Father and the Son. The Son 'looks up to his Father,' gives thanks to him and unites his offering with the Father's gifts of bread and wine. Our offering becomes power of transformation. What is brought as offering from human beings and the life of Christ is borne into the realm of the Father where it is accepted, lifted and transformed. It will now work as a power of transformation in nature, in the realm of the Father-God.

The ability and strength to offer something is not a natural inclination, but emanates from the human soul and its relation to Christ. It is a power which is not found in the realm of the Father, but is only in the human realm and in Christ, the divine being who became human. When the Father-God accepts the offering it becomes objective and a new part of eternal world-being and world-substance.

But it does not simply become part of the original substance of the world, but becomes part of a new world-order of a higher and more spiritualized kind. Nature's gifts of the Father, bread and wine, are lifted into a higher state becoming part of the reality of the union of Father and Son, they become the body and blood of Christ.

The substances of bread and wine are transformed, since the Father-God 'lets live' in them the being and substance of his Son. We can have the image that the Father opens the realm of his kingdom for the Son and raises what comes from the Son into a cornerstone of a new, spiritualized world-existence. And thus at the end of Transubstantiation the words are spoken, 'Let the bread be ...' and 'Let the wind be ...' This is our supplication to the Father-God to elevate human becoming into the realm of his eternal being. Here the help of the Spirit-God is called on, so that the Spirit's 'power of grace' can 'work earthwards' to support the elevation into the realm of eternal spiritual existence.

The entire process, which in the Offering and the first part of the Transubstantiation was addressed to the Father-God, changes to address the community present. Three times the Father-God has been asked to 'receive.' Now those present are twice asked to 'take...' (the bread and the wine), then to 'take this into your thinking' and immediately afterwards, 'thus lives in us.'

We human beings are now the recipients. What has been offered and transformed now returns to human beings and goes through them into the world as a transforming power. A higher nature, a future reality starts to come to birth in earthly reality. This can only come to pass through Christ's power and through the Spirit who is at work in human beings.

During the *Communion* we turn again to Christ. He is repeatedly addressed with the words: 'Thou, O Christ.' The words signify the transformed relationship. His body and his blood are to be taken into our body and blood. But *our* body and blood is not ours alone, for our substance is part of the earth to which we return it when we die. What we receive in the Communion will quite literally stream with our body and blood into the earth. With the help of the Son we plant into the earth a higher reality, the 'medicine everlasting' for the 'sickness of sin' which afflicts all of creation.' What fell into the grasp of the adversary powers is thus wrested back from them and returned to the Trinity. The new creation is no repetition of the old, however — the journey through exile from their origin enables human beings, and with them the created world, to become partners in the creative life of the Trinity.

Conclusion

Looking at the sacraments and the Act of Consecration of Man we have come to the end of our journey. The purpose of the book is not to give interesting and informative facts, but to stimulate and help readers in their search for a meaningful life, and strengthen religious experience and practice.

Bibliography

Auer, Johann, and Joseph Ratzinger, *Kleine Katholische Dogmatik* [concise Catholic dogma], Regensburg 1978.

Frieling, Rudolf, *Christianity and Islam*, Floris Books, Edinburgh 1977.

Nietzsche, Friedrich, *Thus Spoke Zarathustra*, translated by R.J. Hollingdale, Penguin, Harmondsworth.

Steiner, Rudolf, *Cosmic and Human Metamorphoses*, Anthroposophical Publishing Co, London 1926.

—, *The Easter Festival in the Evolution of the Mysteries*, Anthroposophic Press, New York and Rudolf Steiner Press, London 1988.

—, *From Beetroot to Buddhism*, Rudolf Steiner Press, London 1999.

—, *The Mystery of the Trinity and the Mission of the Spirit*, Anthroposophic Press, New York 1991.

—, *Verses and Meditations*, translated by George and Mary Adams, Rudolf Steiner Press, London 1972.

Cosmic Christ

Hans-Werner Schroeder

The question of the cosmic reality of Christ is central to modern Christian awareness. We see lively debate about Christ's nature in relation to the earth and creation, not only within the Church itself but also in more speculative areas of thinking and feeling, such as creation spirituality and the New Age movement.

The works of Teilhard de Chardin and Fritjof Capra have stimulated many to think spiritually about the created world and the part of humankind in its evolution. These issues were also illuminated by Rudolf Steiner in his Christology which placed the Incarnation at a pivotal point of earthly evolution.

Floris Books

Necessary Evil

Hans-Werner Schroeder

Why is there suffering, sickness and death? Why is no corner of human life and society immune from egotism, fear, tyranny, betrayal and guilt? What was God thinking when he allowed evil to come into existence?

Drawing on the worldview of Rudolf Steiner, the author explains that the roots of evil lie with angelic beings. Schroeder discusses evil's prehistory in heaven and shows how the polarity of two kinds of evil, with good as a balance between them, manifests itself in earthly history, and in the areas of education, work, human relationships, sexuality, religion and technology.

With the increased influence of evil in today's world, Schroeder considers how prayer, meditation and angelic guidance through reincarnation give us the possibility to overcome evil in all its forms.

Floris Books

The Rhythm of the Christian Year

Emil Bock

For many people today the intimate connection that exists between the human being and the seasonal rhythms of the year has been lost. Emancipated from nature by the progress of modern technology, we have at the same time become alienated from the earth's cyclical patterns. Our religious life, once so deeply embedded in and supported by the natural world, has increasingly lost awareness of the profound rhythm in the festive year. Only perhaps at Christmas time and at Easter does a vague memory survive of the inter-relationship between earthly and cosmic events.

In this collection of festival meditations, Emil Bock explores ways to deepen our understanding of the Christian festive year. An active renewal of the festivals today can not only heighten our appreciation of the Earth as a living organism, but can provide new energy for humanity's social life. Above all, the festivals are opportunities for new understanding of the Christ mystery that is breaking through in our time — the revelation of Christ in the etheric world.

Floris Books

The Apocalypse of Saint John

Emil Bock

Bock interprets John's rich pictorial language, often found harsh and mysterious, and shows that John is dealing with the universal problems of spiritual development.

This is not just a detailed commentary on the Apocalypse. It is a profound and encouraging examination of human needs in today's world, and shows how we can read the Book of Revelation to understand Christ's position as leader through danger in the present and the future.

Floris Books